TRY THE SPIRITS

Try the Spirits

Christianity and Psychical Research

by

E. Garth Moore

New York

OXFORD UNIVERSITY PRESS

1977

Library of Congress Cataloging in Publication Data

Moore, Evelyn Garth.
  Try the spirits.
  Bibliography: p.
  Includes index.
  1. Psychical research.   2. Christianity and psychical research.
  I. Title.
BF1031.M673   133.8   77-24734
ISBN 0-10-519972-3
ISBN 0-19-519973-1 pbk.

First published in Great Britain in 1977
as *Believe It or Not*
by A. R. Mowbray & Co. Ltd.
Copyright © 1977 A. R. Mowbray & Co. Ltd.
Printed in the United States of America

CONTENTS

APPENDIX

PREFACE

'THERE are more things in heaven and earth, Horatio, than are dreamt of in your philosophy', said Hamlet immediately after he had seen his father's ghost. Such was the effect upon him of his brief encounter with the psychic. There *are* more things in heaven and earth than are dreamt of, or, at least, considered seriously, in the philosophy of many. As a result, their philosophy is defective. Yet a single psychical experience at first hand can suffice to change their attitude and to convince them that there have been serious omissions from the bases upon which their philosophy has been constructed. Those who acknowledge the existence of God recognise that, so far as he is knowable, he is to be known largely by his works, that is, by his Creation. They recognise, therefore, that orthodox science, with its concern for what has been created, is the handmaid of theology, for it tells us something about God. It is not so widely recognised that psychical research also has something to contribute to our knowledge of Creation and, therefore, of God. This is partly because the matters with which psychical research is concerned are so often dismissed as beyond belief. It is against this summary dismissal that this book has been written.

It is intended primarily for those who take the Christian religion seriously without necessarily being themselves either Christians or theologians, and who know little or nothing about psychical research, but who are prepared at least to consider that it is within the bounds of possibility that it might have something of value to contribute, and that the so-called natural sciences do not provide a total view of the picture of which each one of us is a part.

Since the basic book for Christians is the Bible, a number of Biblical references is given. They are, it is hoped, apposite; but it is not to be thought that they are all of the same weight. The differing conclusions of a host of Biblical scholars are not to be ignored, when it comes to assessing the reliability and relative weight of different passages; and this is so, even when, as is sometimes the case, these conclusions are influenced by a materialistic disbelief in the supernormal. But to treat of Biblical criticism adequately in a short introduction to psychical research is impossible and has not been here attempted, save where absolutely necessary. It is, however, worth remarking in passing that some conclusions of some critics concerning the factuality of some Biblical passages might have been different, or, at least, more tentative, if those critics had been better acquainted with psychical research.

Anyone who writes (or publishes) a book on psychical research, especially if he treats of the subject at all favourably, is sticking out his neck and must expect chops at it from a variety of quarters. He is liable to be assailed by spiritualists on the score of incredulity; and by natural scientists for excessive credulity; and by one body of theologians for taking Biblical statements too literally; and by another body of theologians for not taking them sufficiently at their face-value. These are hazards which he must accept, particularly if he attempts a purely introductory work which does not admit of an examination of many of the issues in the depth which they demand and which he would like to accord them. This book, being purely introductory, is, therefore, superficially vulnerable to such attacks. That does not mean that, in a more extensive work, the attacks could not be repulsed.

Psychic phenomena are unusual, though much more common than is often imagined. Being unusual, unusually strong evidence is required to satisfy us that they have occurred. The main object of this book is to be descriptive, and, therefore, no attempt has been made to muster the evidence to support the phenomena described. Examples, however, are given to illustrate these phenomena, some of them from my own experience. The fact that, as presented here, they fail to come up to the stringent evidential requirements of psychical research is recognised. But that does not detract from their value as typical examples of the sorts of phenomena that occur. The reader who wishes to pursue the subject further and to satisfy himself that such things really do occur will find plenty of well-attested evidence in the literature on the subject, and, to assist him, a guide to further reading is given in the Appendix.

No claim is made on behalf of this book to originality, save possibly in some aspects of its presentation and in some of the ideas suggested. Beyond that minute contribution, it adds nothing to the body of research into the subject. Its purpose is to make that research more widely known and its implications more seriously considered.

Since in a subject such as this the reader is entitled to information about everything which may assist him towards a fair assessment, the predispositions of the author are a matter upon which he should be informed.

Briefly, then, while I have considerable reservations about some of the claims which are made, I do accept as proved a number of psychical phenomena, notably telepathy, precognition, apparitions and poltergeists. For this reason, though theologically no fundamentalist, I am less prone than are some 'rational' critics to incredulity concerning the miracles recorded in the Bible. The explanation of psychic phenomena, Biblical or modern, is another matter, and I seek to discover the relationship of proved psychic phenomena to the whole body of knowledge which the natural sciences provide, and I seek to relate the totality of our knowledge to that basic Christianity upon which I firmly take my stand as being supported by experience and rooted in reason, though transcending understanding and most certainly not beyond belief.

I

INTRODUCTION

'HAVE *you* ever seen a ghost?' I said to a boy of about twelve who was discussing the subject with a companion of about the same age. I asked the question more with a view to ending the conversation than with anything else in mind, for parents are not always keen on children's discussing such matters, and I was temporarily *in loco parentis*. The boy's reply, however, was striking and unexpected. 'I don't know,' he said, contemplatively, 'but I think so.' This was too much for my inquisitiveness and, throwing quasi-parental obligations to the wind, I asked for details, which he gave clearly and with impressive simplicity.

It appears that he had been going home along a straight stretch of road in Suffolk. It was evening, but still light. The road was bounded by high hedges on each side with no turning off and it was empty save for the boy and a man who was walking some twenty yards ahead of the boy. Suddenly the man was there no longer. The boy was puzzled and looked to see where the man could have turned off into the fields; but he could find no such place. The next day, in the middle of the day, the boy returned to the road and went over the whole stretch of it, still seeking for somewhere where the man could have gone, until he was satisfied that there was in fact no way off. The boy felt driven to the conclusion that there had been no such man the evening before and that what he had seen was a ghost.

To anyone acquainted with psychical research, the story will come as no surprise. There are plenty more like it. All that was unusual about the story was the admirably scientific attitude displayed by the boy, an attitude worthy of a psychical researcher.

Psychical research *is* a science, albeit a young one and one which is only just beginning to be accepted as respectable. It is not easy to define its limits; but it is important to say at the outset what it is not. It is not spiritism, or, as it is more usually called, spiritualism. Spiritualism is a kind of religion of which the outstanding feature is belief in survival of bodily death and the active pursuit of what its devotees believe is genuine communication with the dead. The phenomena in which spiritualists are interested are also of interest to the psychical researcher (and a spiritualist may also be a researcher); but the psychical researcher does not necessarily, or, indeed usually, place the same value on these phenomena as does the spiritualist, nor does he so readily accept them at their face-value, and, further, he is interested in a much wider range of phenomena.

It is the very width of this range that makes it difficult to define or delimit the subject. Ghosts are certainly included within this range. So are the alleged communications through mediums upon which spiritualists place so much store. But so also are telepathy (the apparent transference of thought from one individual to another), precognition (foreseeing the future), telekinesis (the movement of objects at a distance by will-power alone), poltergeist-phenomena (the apparent manifestatation of noisy and mischievous entities which also move physical objects), hypnotism, out-of-the-body experiences, clairvoyance and clairaudience, materialisation (of persons and objects in the séance room) apports (the transference of objects from one place to another, sometimes through walls), possession, and perhaps much else which is unusual. In short, it is tempting to describe the objects of psychical research as anything unusual about which little is known. The common factor between them is that they all, if genuine, appear to run counter to the known laws of physics. This accounts for the scepticism with which for so long the subject has been regarded by natural scientists. It also helps to account for the fact that natural scientists are beginning to look on psychical research with a more kindly eye and with greater interest than was once the case. What were once regarded as the firmly based and all-embracing laws of nature are now recognised by scientists as sufficient only within a limited context, but as inadequate expression of the whole truth. For example, Einstein's theory of relativity has played havoc with many preconceived ideas. With this growing realisation that the laws of nature are far wider than was once believed, there has come a greater readiness to accept the fact that psychic phenomena do exist and are, therefore, worth studying.

Serious psychical research is only about a hundred years old. During these hundred years some progress has been made in psychical research; but the progress has not been fast. This is partly due to the fact that psychical researchers have quite rightly sought to be strictly scientific and have, therefore, employed techniques appropriate to the natural sciences, but not necessarily the right ones for psychical research. In many respects we have yet to find the right techniques. A pint-pot is an admirable vessel for measuring beer; but it is not well adapted to measuring electricity. It is difficult to find the right techniques for assessing psychical phenomena, especially the spontaneous phenomena. How does one establish the veridical nature of an apparition? What, in fact, do we mean by the word *veridical*? *The Concise Oxford Dictionary* defines it as 'Truthful . . . coinciding with reality'. In the case of an apparition, the viewer believes that he is seeing something, and, if a photograph also reveals something, a measure of corroboration is provided and we say that the vision was veridical. If, however, the photograph reveals nothing, there must still be *some* cause, albeit internal to the viewer, giving rise to the impression. If the cause is entirely internal to the viewer, we say that the vision is not veridical. By 'coinciding with reality' we presumably mean that, whether or not there be corroboration, we can trace something external to the viewer which links with what he has seen.

Some would-be researchers, too, have been alienated by the amount of fraud which investigations have revealed. It is certainly tiresome to have to be constantly on one's guard against, not only fraud, but also the subsequent suggestion that there was room for fraud. But the existence of false coins, though it makes all currency suspect, does not detract from the value of the undoubtedly true coin.

The natural scientist who has scoffed at psychical research has often found allies in an unexpected, and at times to him unwelcome quarter. Organised religion of many sorts has tended to be hostile. This is something which is treated more fully in Chapters 9, 10 and 11. Here it is simply to be noted as a factor which has caused some to fight shy of the subject.

The purpose of this book is to stress the importance of psychical research in the hope that it may be taken seriously both by those who are interested in religion and also by those who are interested in the natural sciences, without, in either case, being necessarily expert in any branch of those two disciplines. It is assumed that the reader has but little knowledge of psychic matters and it is hoped that the brief account here given of some of the aspects of psychical research may sufficiently whet the appetites of some readers to cause them to turn to fuller works on the subject. Since it is impossible in the short compass of this book to treat of every aspect of psychical research or to do more than introduce the subject, little attempt has been made here to substantiate by evidence many of the statements contained in this book.

At the outset, however, certain points require to be made.

The first is that we are dealing in large measure with facts and not just with old wives' tales. That there is plenty of fiction, and, indeed, of fraud, is not denied. But, beneath it all, is a hard substratum of fact, and this, it is hoped, will become apparent to the reader who is persuaded to turn to some of the books listed in the Appendix. It is to my mind idle to deny the fact of telepathy; its explanation is quite another matter. It is idle to deny the fact of precognition; its explanation is even more baffling and raises the profoundest problems about predetermination and, indeed, about the very nature of time. Poltergeist-activities have disturbed far too many humdrum households to be dismissed as mere figments of the imagination; but what precisely a poltergeist is still remains to be discovered. Right down the ages persons have seen and heard and even felt ghosts, and some of the cases are too well authenticated to let one dismiss all the remainder as fantasy; but what a ghost is (and there may be several different sorts of ghosts) is still a matter for investigation.

If it once be granted that some psychical phenomena are facts (even though some be fictional), then it is obvious that they are very important facts. In the realm of natural science they call for a reassessment of much that has been taken for granted. They call for a restatement of many of the so-called natural laws (such as, that two bodies cannot occupy the same space at the same time), or else for a realisation that these laws as at present formulated provide an inadequate picture of the Universe. In the realm of religion they at least provide support for religion's basic contention that the material world around us is not the whole of Creation. They in fact provide corroborative (though not conclusive) evidence for much else besides (see Chapter 11).

Even if it were conclusively shown (which it could not be) that all psychic phenomena were imaginary or fraudulent, they would still provide intriguing examples of self-deception and of other matters for psychological discussion or examples of skilful deception and of expert, though misguided, manipulation.

Psychical research is, therefore, something which deserves the serious attention of serious-minded persons, and it can employ the skills of the natural scientist, the psychologist, the physician, the conjurer, the detective and the theolgian. Not everyone, however, should aspire to become a researcher, and none should dabble irresponsibly (see p. 115 *et. seq.*). But the results obtained by researchers are open to all and can scarcely fail to widen the horizons of those who read them.

2

TELEPATHY

PSYCHICAL research contains much that is dramatic and much that is boring. Hauntings are dramatic; and statistically supported, oft-repeated experiments in thought-transference can be very boring. While it is tempting to begin with the dramatic, it is as well to resist the temptation and to begin with telepathy and pre-cognition. These are not without their dramatic content. But the reason for beginning with them is that evident-ially they are well attested and, further, as will become apparent later (see Chapter 4), they provide material which must be taken into account when seeking to interpret other psychical phenomena.

Telepathy is the apparent conveyance of thought from one person to another without the intervention of any known physical means. It can be deliberate, when the sender and the receiver set themselves to the tasks of sending and receiving messages, ideas, thoughts or pictures, and it has been the subject of many laboratory experiments. It can also occur, when the sender attempts to convey a thought to a receiver who does not know that the attempt is being made. It can occur, too, when a receiver sets himself to pick up the thoughts of another who is unaware that anyone is trying to read his mind. It can be spontaneous, when the receiver seems to get an idea from the mind of another, when that other is not seeking to transmit anything and when the receiver is not consciously seeking to pick up anything. Some accounts of spontaneous telepathy are, if not dramatic, highly intriguing and are possibly examples of clairvoyance,[1] or of something akin to it, rather than of telepathy. For this reason such phenomena and telepathy (if they be different), together with any acquisition of knowledge other than by physical means, has come to be called extra-sensory perception, usually abbreviated to ESP.

There is evidence of it in the Bible, where it is stated (Luke 6. 7, 8) that Jesus knew the thoughts of the scribes and Pharisees, and possibly in the statement (John 2. 24–5) that 'he needed not that any should testify of a man: for he knew what was in man'; and again (John 6. 60–1), 'When Jesus knew in himself that his disciples murmured'. If these are example of telepathy, examples of a kindred ESP are to be found in our Lord's supernormal knowledge of the history of the woman of Samaria (John 4) and when he 'saw' Nathanael under the fig-tree.[2] In both these last two cases each of his hearers appears to have regarded the phenomenon as dramatic. The woman of Samaria went off and told her neighbours to come and see a man who had told her everything which she had ever done—a gross exaggeration, but one which need not surprise us for there are many modern examples of such exaggeration, and, for this reason, her reaction encourages credence in the story. Nathanael was so impressed by Jesus's exhibition of ESP that he exclaimed, 'Rabbi, thou art the Son of God; thou art the King of Israel!' a conclusion which, even though right, did not necessarily follow, as our Lord was quick to point out when he replied, 'Because I said unto thee, "I saw thee under the fig tree", believest thou? Thou shalt see greater things than these.'

But to come to modern times: Mrs Rosalind Heywood, a noted and acute psychical researcher, but also almost certainly herself a sensitive (that is, one with a psychic faculty), gives interesting accounts of her *rapport* with her husband (*The Infinite Hive*, by Rosalind Heywood, Pan Books Ltd, 35p, pp. 111 *et seq.*). It seems to be a two-way traffic. She relates how her husband mentally summoned her to come to him—a deliberate act on his part. She relates how, when he was in need of a torch, she felt and responded to the urge to go to the station with one to meet him. This was not in response to a consciously sent message, but in response to a need. It may, therefore, not be strictly a case of telepathy, but it is an example of ESP akin to telepathy, namely, an awareness of something without any of the physical aids to awareness.

Dr Gilbert Murray, the well-known classical scholar, believed himself to be the recipient of many consciously transmitted telepathic messages (see *Proceedings of the SPR* (Society for Psychical Research), vol. XXIX, pp. 46 *et seq.*, vol. XLIX, pp. 155 *et seq.*, and vol. XXXIX, pp. 212 *et seq.*). He would go out of, and away from, the room while those left behind would agree on some thought to be transmitted. Murray would then return to the room and make his guess as to what had been decided, apparently with a large measure of startling success. The targets set him were sometimes very recondite; such as Jane Eyre's being stood on a stool at school and being accused of lying. They were seldom other than far removed from the immediate scene. One was a thought by his daughter of herself dancing at The Hague with the head of the Dutch Foreign Office, which Murray interpreted as a journey abroad and a sort of official soirée or dancing in Holland. Unfortunately none of these domestic experiments was conducted under satisfactory test conditions. There is no reason whatever to doubt the integrity of either Gilbert Murray or his family and friends, though there are some who would accept the hypothesis of fraud rather than that of ESP. But it has been suggested that a possible alternative explanation is hyperaesthesia on Murray's part, that is, a greatly heightened acuity of hearing. Murray himself eventually became aware of this possibility. It seems highly improbable; but, if true, it is almost as remarkable as genuine telepathy. Under strict test conditions great care is taken to exclude any possibility of information's being conveyed through any of the five ordinary senses, and since the conditions under which Murray operated were not strict test conditions, some reservations must be made, even by those who are disposed to accept that Murray displayed great powers of telepathic receptivity.

Telepathy, however, lends itself singularly well to laboratory experiments under strict test conditions, and many such experiments have been conducted with significant statistical results. One of the methods used is card-guessing, especially with a pack of Zener cards, which are thought to be more satisfactory than ordinary playing cards. Each card bears a single symbol, and there are five symbols, namely, a square, a circle, a cross, three wavy lines and a star. There are twenty-five cards in a pack—five of each symbol. In its simplest form the experiment consists of one person (the agent) who looks at one of the cards, while another person (the percipient) guesses which one it is. Under the strictest possible conditions so as to preclude any possibility of the percipient's acquiring knowledge of the card by ordinary means, with some agents and percipients, success has been far beyond chance.

Many other types of laboratory experiment have been conducted. One of the most striking was with simple pictures and is known as the Guthrie Experiment (*Proceedings of the SPR*, vol. II). The agent drew a simple device and the percipient was asked to reproduce it. There were six of them, and, if the reader will compare the originals drawn by the agent with the copies made by the percipient, he will see for himself how strikingly successful this experiment appears to be.

Originals

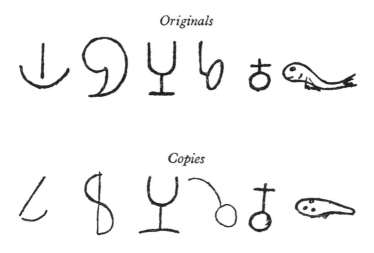

Copies

Fig. 1 'A complete consecutive series of six drawings transmitted by telepathy from Mr Guthrie to Miss E without contact during the Liverpool experiment. . . . When No. 6 was being transmitted, Miss E said almost directly, "Are you thinking of the bottom of the sea, with shell and fishes?" and then, "Is it a snail or a fish?" – then drew as above.'

Proceedings SPR, Vol. II

3
PRECOGNITION

PRECOGNITION (knowing the future) is one of the most puzzling as well as one of the most common of psychic phenomena. It is so common that it is suspected that everybody has the experience, but does not always recognise it. It seems to occur more often, but by no means exclusively, in dreams. It is thought to be sometimes the explanation of the sensation which many have at some time experienced of *déjà vu*—the sensation of having been to a place before, or of having been in a situation before, often accompanied by the odd, but very brief, feeling, immediately justified, of knowing what is going to happen next. The suggestion is that one has previewed the experience in a dream which one has forgotten, but the memory of which has been stored in the subconscious.

I will give three brief personal experiences of my own to illustrate what is under discussion, two of them examples of precognition in dreams and one of them a waking experience. In one of them I was the object of the experience and in the other two I was the percipient. None of them is evidential, for they rest solely on my word. But, since the reader can and should test the reality of precognition for himself (see p. 18) there is no need to burden this introductory book with evidence.

In the first experience the young woman who was then our cook was the percipient. I came into the kitchen one afternoon holding out a bunch of giant radishes which I had just pulled up from the garden. As I did so, the cook exclaimed, 'Why, that's my dream!' When I asked for an explanation, she said, 'Last night I dreamt that you came in, just like that, with a bunch of turnips in your hand.' (Radishes are a kind of turnip and, from a short distance, a bunch of giant radishes might well be mistaken for a bunch of turnips.) So far as I am aware, this cook is no more psychic than the average run of persons, and her experience is typical of that which many persons have.

I, too, make no claim to being psychic; but I had the following experience. I dreamt that I was standing in a part of the house which was known as the laundry, because it had a large copper in it and had obviously once been used for that purpose. It also contained a large bin into which I used to put the potatoes from the garden. In my dream I was standing by this bin, when the cook (the same one) came in and said, 'I do wish you wouldn't bring me so many little potatoes. They are so difficult to peel.' On the morning immediately following my dream, I was putting on my gardening-shoes which I had left near the laundry and, while I was doing so, I remembered my dream. That made me think that I had better look at the potato-bin to see whether I ought to bring up some more potatoes from the garden. In consequence I went into the laundry and was looking at the contents of the bin, when the cook came in and said, 'I do wish you wouldn't bring me so many little potatoes. They are so difficult to peel.' This tale, though simple, has a complicating factor in that, to some extent, the dream seems to have contributed to its own fulfilment.[1] It is quite likely that I should have gone to the bin in any event, and almost certain that I should have done so at some time in order to see whether more potatoes were needed. But the immediate cause of my going at that moment was the recollection of my dream, though, when I did so, I was not anticipating the encounter with the cook.

My third case is a waking experience, and it is possibly not really a case of precognition. It could be explained psychologically as the externalisation of a sub-conscious observance of the passage of time. But precognition can also explain it (at least, in so far as the inexplicable can be said to provide an explanation.) It took place in a provincial city during the Assizes. If everything had gone according to plan, I should have been in Court. But something went wrong with the cause-list and my case was postponed to the next day. I thus found myself with time to kill and I went off on a church-crawl. I had been into a number of churches and I had lost count of time and I had no watch. Actually, most of us do not lose *all* count of time, and our awareness of the passage of time (including our ability to wake up at a pre-appointed time) is itself a phenomenon worth studying. But on this occasion I do not think that I knew the time within a couple of hours. As I strolled along the street I was looking out for a public clock. Suddenly I saw one, or, rather I thought I did, and it registered ten minutes to six. But, as I looked at it, the clock-face faded away and I found myself staring at a circular blank ornamental plaque on the side of a building. Somewhat puzzled, I strolled on for about two minutes (note that) until I came to an undoubted public clock which did not fade away and was in a post-office. It registered 6.52.

These three cases are all of trivial incidents and as

such they are not untypical. There are recorded cases of the precognition of important, often catastrophic, events, such as the Aberfan disaster (see SPR *Journal* (Dec. 1967), vol. 44). But the majority of cases are of trivial events. When the precognition occurs in a dream, it is by no means an exact forecast of the subsequent event, but near enough to be recognised. It would seem that, just as our dreams are often recognisable as containing jumbled recollections of the past, so they also contain jumbled anticipations of the future.

What does this ability to foretell the future signify? It is an intriguing and disturbing question. Does it indicate that everything is predetermined? It certainly lends force to the more extreme forms of Calvinism and to the Calvinistic doctrine of predestination. It is not a popular doctrine, for we like to think that we are, to some extent at least, master of our fate, and to hold that the course of events is predetermined seems to make a mockery of all endeavour, human or otherwise. The acceptance of predetermination does not necessarily lead to the conclusion that all events are predetermined. They may be; but it is logically possible to conceive of a Creator who predetermines some things and has the ability to ensure the fulfilment of his plans, but who, within the framework of what he has chosen to predetermine, leaves a range of choice to his creatures. One can conceive of an architect who has prepared an outline master-plan, but who has left the details to be filled in by others. But such a concept fits uneasily with the idea of predetermination concerning trivialities, such as the pulling-up of radishes or complaints about the size of potatoes.

There are, however, to my mind two ways in which one can accept precognition as a fact and yet avoid the conclusion of predetermination. They are not mutually

exclusive, for, while each alone suffices to avoid that conclusion, they may both on occasions operate.

The first is best illustrated by the well-known analogy
of a man standing on the top of a hill round the base of
which runs a single railway-track. From his vantage-
point he sees two trains approaching one another. He
can see them both; but the drivers of the two trains (and
the passengers) are hidden from each other by the curve
of the hill. It does not require much acumen on the part
of the observer on the hill-top to foresee at least the
probability of a collision. The collision is not, however,
inevitable. The drivers may see each other in time to
brake, or the observer himself may be able to intervene
by giving some sort of warning, thus utilising his foresight
and by doing so, playing some part in shaping the future.
In other words, someone possessed of sufficient relevant
data can foretell the probable course of future events,
and even intervene to shape them.

Another illustration is provided by the type of
prophecy exhibited by the prophets of the Old Testament. By reason of their holiness they were better
attuned than were their contemporaries to the will of
God; they were more aware than their contemporaries of
the extent to which the nation had departed from that
will; and they saw more clearly the probable consequences of such departure. That is why so much of their
prophecy takes the form of denunciation of the present
as well as warning concerning the future. For the purpose
of illustrating this type of prophecy, it is not necessary
to import the concept of holiness or of the will of God.
All that is required to mark out the prophet from his less
gifted contemporaries is that he should possess a more
lively appreciation of the present situation and a better
judgement as to the probable consequences. Winston

Churchill was a prophet, when, between the two world wars, he warned us that Germany was preparing for another tiger-spring at our throats. More clearly than his contemporaries he read the signs of the times and interpreted the outcome with accuracy. Like so many prophets, he was ignored, for his hearers did not wish to see such an outcome or to take the steps necessary to avoid it, and there are none so deaf as those who will not hear. But the future was not necessarily predetermined. His warnings could have been heeded and appropriate action taken to avert the threatened catastrophe.

The second way in which one can accept precognition as a fact and yet avoid the conclusion of predeterminism depends on a particular concept of the nature of time. It is one which we can just, but only just, grasp intellectually, but which we are quite incapable of truly envisaging. It adumbrates that time is part of God's Creation, and that, just as he stands outside the rest of his Creation, so also does he stand outside time. Time so conceived is, as it were, a cage within which the rest of Creation (or, at least, of the material Creation) is imprisoned; or perhaps it should be likened, not to a cage, but to a shelter wherein the rest of the material Creation is protected. For God, time, as we know it, does not exist, or, rather, has no influence. All time is (as we are forced to say) going on at the same time. For God, the Creation, the Crucifixion and the Last Judgement are all present together in one eternal flash. For us, however, time is something along which we flow, or which flows past us, and everything which is not the immediate present is either past or future. It is a concept of time which can be expressed mathematically and has been so expressed by the Oxford engineer, the late J. W. Dunne, in his two books *An Experiment with Time* (1st edn.,

Faber, London, 1927) and *The Serial Universe* (Faber, London, 1934) in which he treats time as a further dimension.

Dunne's mathematics (which the late Professor Eddington described as sound, while reserving judgement as to Dunne's conclusions) may be too indigestible for the reader who is not mathematically minded; but the opening chapters of *An Experiment with Time* may profitably and without effort be read by all. They should certainly be read by those who find precognition interesting. Dunne gives examples of precognitive experiences, especially in dreams, and urges his readers to have handy by the bedside a pencil and paper. As soon as he wakes up, whether in the middle of the night or in the morning, he should *immediately* jot down as much of his dream as he can remember. To do so at once is important, as, however vivid the dream may have been, for some reason, which merits further investigation, the recollection of it so often quickly vanishes. Dunne maintains that dreams thus recorded have frequently a precognitive content. My own experience endorses this so fully that, after a short while, I gave up the chore of thus recording my dreams (for it *is* a boring chore), being satisfied that, for me at least, what Dunne says is true. It is something which each reader can test for himself. If any reader who takes the test gets only negative results, let him remember that with others the results are positive, and that, therefore, precognition is a fact, albeit not yet convincingly explained.

It is a fact, whatever be its explanation. It is a fact, moreover, which must be taken into account, together with telepathy, when considering other types of psychical phenomena (see Chapter 4). It is a fact which must be taken into account when considering telepathy. In the last chapter reference was made to card-guessing as a laboratory test for telepathy. During some of these experiments something very interesting occurred. It looked as though some percipients, when taking part in a series of runs through the cards, were scoring very badly. Then the results were scrutinised more closely and it was found that, far from scoring badly, they were scoring well; but they were not scoring on the current target-card; they were scoring instead on two or three cards ahead. They were scoring, not on the card at which the agent was then looking, but on the one at which he was going to look two or three turns later. It looked as though precognition had somehow crept into the experiment uninvited and had ousted straightforward telepathy. that, indeed, may be what had happened; but it has happened fairly frequently and it raises the question of whether it happens more frequently than we suspect; whether, in fact, what appears to be telepathy may, at least sometimes, be precognition in disguise. In any event, in these cases, a *psi* faculty was being exhibited by someone—by the percipient or by the agent or by both (a *psi* faculty is one of a psychic nature).

Dr J. E. Ormes suggests (SPR *Journal*, vol. 47, No. 760 (June 1974)) that possibly precognition is at the root of a number of psychic phenomena which look like something else. But to confine ourselves for the moment to card-guessing: after a run or a number of runs through the cards has been made, it is necessary, in order to complete the experiment to go through the scores which have been recorded. This involves going through the record of the cards at which the agent has looked and comparing it with the record of guesses which the percipient has made. It is logically possible that, instead of registering a card which the agent was seeking to indicate by telepathy, what the percipient has unwittingly done is to precognise either a card which is soon to be turned up or else the final list of those which have been turned up. It is logically possible; but we are as yet too ignorant to know whether it is probable. All that we can say with any degree of certainty is that it looks as though the time-factor is one which we must take into account far more seriously than we have done in what we commonly call the past.

4

MEDIUMSHIP AND SÉANCES

MEDIUMSHIP is of particular interest to spiritualists, because a medium is someone who purports to be in communication with what they call 'the world of spirit' and especially with the spirits of the departed, and belief in the possibility of such communication is the most prominent feature in spiritualism. The activities of mediums are, however, also of interest to psychical researchers, whether the researcher be himself a spiritualist or not; for whether or not one accepts the spiritualists' interpretation of the phenomena exhibited by mediums, there can be little doubt that a genuine medium exhibits the *psi* (or psychic) faculty in greater or less degree. *Psi* is the term commonly employed to denote any faculty which appears not to depend on the physical. Every genuine medium is, therefore, a sensitive; but every sensitive is not a medium. A person may, for example, be a good recipient of telepathic communications without ever attempting mediumship. It is probable, however, that any sensitive could, if he wished, develop powers which would exhibit themselves in the same way as do those of mediums. If, then, a medium be really one who is in touch with the world of spirit, it may well be that any sensitive could himself get in touch with that world.

The question is whether that is what genuine mediums

really do. There have undoubtedly been fraudulent mediums; but there have been, and are, many who are absolutely honest, and, indeed, dedicated, persons who exhibit genuine psychic phenomena. It is with them that we are primarily concerned, and we are concerned to discover whether their apparent communications with the unseen world are what the mediums themselves genuinely believe them to be, or whether they are susceptible to some other interpretation.

Mediums are to be found in both sexes; but women predominate. Whether this indicates that this type of sensitivity is more common in women than in men, or whether it is simply a sociological reflection has yet to be determined. It may well be simply that there are more women than men with time to spare, and that professional mediumship provides a way by which widows and other women of slender means can supplement an exiguous income.

Their method of working varies considerably; but most give séances to the bereaved and to others who are seeking communication with some particular deceased person or persons. It is very common for the medium to go into trance, either light or profound. In this condition some mediums appear to have their bodies taken over or possessed by some extraneous intelligent entity who speaks through the medium, often in a noticeably different voice. Other mediums, however, seem to retain their own identity and purport to tell the sitter (the client) what the medium pyschically sees or hears. But some mediums do not seem to go into trance at all or into only a very light trance. It is possible, however, that all mediums in fact go into a least a very light trance, so light that it is scarcely noticeable to the onlooker, for they seem to have the faculty of switching on and off at will, and it may be that what we call 'switching on' is simply the voluntary induction of a very light trance. Those who appear to go into a trance of any depth, especially those who seem in that state to be possessed by another entity, usually claim, when they come out of trance, to have no knowledge whatever of what went on while they were in trance. The precise nature of a trance is not yet known; but it may well be the result of self-hypnosis.

Among those who do not appear to go into trance at all or into only a very light trance, the use of the ouija-board or resort to automatic writing is not uncommon. A ouija-board consists of a board of highly polished wood, about eighteen inches by twelve inches, with the letters of the alphabet inscribed on it, together with the numerals and sometimes with the words *yes*, *no* and *and*. (The outlandish word, *ouija* (pronounced *wee-jah*), is a combination of the French *oui* and the German *ja* and presumably comes from the word *yes* inscribed on the board.) Upon this board is placed a wooden pointer about five inches long, one inch broad and one inch thick, the pointer having a felt base so that it may slide easily over the surface of the board. On this pointer the medium lightly places the fingers of one hand and usually invites the sitter simultaneously to do the same. If the experiment is successful, the pointer then moves about over the board, apparently of its own violation and often with remarkable rapidity, and spells out messages and answers to questions. It seems to be a more efficient method of getting results than the use of the planchette, which is a heart-shaped piece of flat wood, mounted at its base on two small wheels of about half an inch diameter and having at its apex a pencil pointing downwards. The planchette is then placed on a sheet of paper and the fingers are placed on the planchette and the planchette then begins to write. In automatic writing, however, the medium simply holds a pencil which proceeds to write apparently undirected by the mind of the medium.

In most such sittings, the séance usually takes place in a good light, though trance-mediums prefer it not to be to bright. There is, however, a further type of medium, known as a physical medium, who usually operates in darkness, relieved only by a dim red light. Such mediums purport to produce physical effects, such as the materialisation of objects like flowers, and even of human forms, these materialisations being said to be formed out of a substance known as ectoplasm which appears in the dim red light to be exuded from the medium's body, especially from the mouth. At such séances other events sometimes take place, such as the movement of objects, and especially, in the case of so-called direct-voice mediums, the movement round the room of a trumpet through which a deceased person, or other discarnate entity audibly speaks, or so it is claimed.

No more will be said here about physical mediumship. It is comparatively rare and, though dramatic, it is obviously susceptible to trickery and, for its proper investigation, calls for the knowledge of a competent conjurer. The darkness and the strict conditions imposed by such mediums on their sitters are such that only the very experienced researcher is in a position to pass any judgement on them. The other types of mediumship provide a simpler, more pleasant and much more fruitful field for investigation, for, beyond taking obvious precautions to ensure that the medium is not apprised by normal means of relevant information, one is concerned at the sitting only with the content of the medium's message and afterwards with its evaluation.

In a typical, well-conducted sitting, the sitter will have taken care to book his appointment with the medium anonymously. He will take care not to reveal his identity and not to drop clues during the sitting which could assist the medium. Indeed, the medium herself, on first seeing the client, is quite likely to give him this warning. She may or she may not dim the light in the room so that there is no glare, and she is probably keen that extraneous noises should be reduced to a minimum, for it would seem that many mediums are, during a sitting, subject to hyperaesthesia so that every noise appears exaggeratedly loud. What happens thereafter depends on the medium's method of working, on whether she goes into trance, deep or light, on whether she is clairvoyante or clairaudient, on whether she remains herself or appears to be taken over by another entity, and so on. One thing that the sitter is likely to find is that, at least in the early stages of a sitting, the medium does not profess to be in direct communication with the deceased person whom the sitter has come to meet. Instead, she claims to be in touch with an entity whom she calls her guide. It is primarily with her spirit-guide that she is in touch, and only through him, with other discarnate entities. Just as on this earth a medium is necessary to effect a link with other states of being, so, out of this earth, a spirit-guide is thought by many to be necessary to effect a link with the medium. So runs the theory. Whether spirit-guides really exist or not is another matter. The medium probably thinks that her guide exists and, for her, he is very real. He may be a deceased human, or he may be pure spirit and he not only acts as an intermediary in the chain between the sitter and some particular deceased person, he also acts as the protector and adviser of the medium, keeping evil influences away from her and acting as a sort of door-keeper who lets through only the particular deceased who is being sought, while excluding other spirit-beings who are anxious to use the medium as a channel of communication.

He would be a rash person who affirmed dogmatically that spirit-guides do not exist; but they often appear to be no more than honest dramatisations created by the medium's own imagination, and they often appear to accord singularly closely with the medium's own degree of sophistication. A sophisticated medium will have a sophisticated guide whose utterances are, like hers, of some intellectual worth. An unsophisticated medium will have an unsophisticated guide who gives voice, through her, to the most banal of platitudes. A large number of guides are said by their mediums to be Red Indians. This may well be due to the fact that modern mediumship was in vogue in America towards the end of the nineteenth century when there were more Red Indians, and these were romanticised and had attributed to them a variety of psychic gifts. It would seem that a fashion was then established among American mediums which was later followed by mediums in this country and still persists, particularly among the less sophisticated mediums.

But the proof of the pudding is in the eating. Interesting and important as are the mechanics of mediumship, the first matter to determine is whether mediums deliver the goods; in other words, what is the quality of the material which comes through them? Often it is trivial and unimpressive. But often it is very impressive, so much so that, on a superficial view, it would seem to establish survival after death. It is the assurance of survival that so many sitters seek. This accounts for the boost in spiritualism which followed in the wake of the great slaughter which occurred during the Great War of

1914–18. Unfortunately for the comfort of those who thirst for this assurance it cannot be said that the séance-room has provided it. It has made survival appear more probable; but it has not conclusively established it. Let us see why not.

Let us suppose that a sitter has gone anonymously to a medium who purports to put him in touch, through her (and perhaps her guide), with his deceased aunt. If he has wits about him (and many sitters have not), he seeks some evidence that it really is his aunt who has come through. Let us suppose that she gives her own name and his correctly (and names seem to come through only with difficulty). Let us suppose that she then relates trivial incidents in the past which he remembers and which it is reasonable to suppose that she would remember. If the incidents are trivial, it is absurd to imagine that the medium could have known anything about them. The sitting may now be claimed as a successful sitting and the sitter may feel justified in concluding that his aunt really has survived death and that he has been in touch with her. Who, other than his aunt, could have described these incidents.

Unfortunately for the hypothesis of survival it is at this point that telepathy has to be taken into account. It may be improbable, but it is logically a possibility, that the medium has never been in touch with the deceased aunt, but has unwittingly picked up telepathically from the mind of the sitter all the information which she has just imparted.

When the sitter becomes aware of this logically possible alternative, let us suppose that he makes another attempt to establish his aunt's survival. This time, when he goes to the medium and the medium purports to get in touch once again with his aunt, he asks his aunt, through the medium, to tell him something which he does not know, but which he can subsequently verify. Let us suppose that the aunt obliges and tells him that, if he goes to the attic in what was her house, he will find a black trunk in the corner, in which there is a casket containing letters, of which he has never before heard, written by his grand-mother. After the séance he goes to his aunt's old house and finds the trunk and the casket and the letters, just as his aunt has said. Here, at last, he may think, is proof of her survival. The medium could not have read his thoughts on the subject, because he knew nothing of the existence of the trunk, the casket and the letters. Tele-pathy as an explanation has been scotched. True; but at this point a second possible explanation suggests itself, namely precognition. It seems highly improbable, but it is a logical possibility, that what the medium has done is to precognise what the sitter was about to do, and did in fact do, after the sitting was over.

⌐Neither telepathy nor precognition may appear to be at all likely explanations; but it seems impossible utterly to exclude them; and it must be remembered that a communication from the dead is, in the opinion of many, equally or more improbable. The one thing which seems to have been proved irrefutably is the abnormal sensitivity of the medium. Either she has really been in touch with the dead, or she has the ability to pick up thoughts telepathically, or she has the gift of precogni-tion. ⌐ In any event, the argument for survival is strengthened, even though it be not conclusively proved. It is strengthened because it has been established that the medium is the recipient of information which comes to her by no known physical means. This indicates that there is in us, or at least in some of us, something more than the purely physical. We can call this something more by any name we like; we can call it the psychic or the spiritual. Call it what we will, it shows that a purely materialistic view of existence is not justified. Once that is established, it becomes more probable that man is not wholly material; and from that it follows that the whole of man does not necessarily perish, when the material part of him decays. The part that remains is the nonphysical.

Apart from the seeming improbability in many séances of the operation of telepathy or precognition, there are other indications tending to show that, at least sometimes, the communications received by the medium really do come from the deceased person from whom they are claimed to come. It has been known for communications to come in a foreign language unknown to both the medium and the sitter. There are times when, undefinably, the personality of a deceased person has come through in a manner impressive to the sitter, though it is something which he can only ask others to take on trust. Most impressive of all, however, have been certain types of communication which bear all the marks of having been carefully devised by an intelligent communicator in order to establish his identity.

High among the last must be ranked those prolonged cases known as cross-correspondence. In essence, cross-correspondence consists of a number of communications purporting to come from the same communicator or band of communicators, and transmitted through different mediums at different times, no single communication taken in isolation making much sense, but all, when assembled together, conveying a message. It is as though a living person were to write a letter, cut it up into several sections and then post each section to a different recipient. It is not until all the sections are collected and put together that the full purport of the letter becomes apparent. The interesting feature of this cross-correspondence is that it is clearly an experiment aimed at establishing survival and it is an experiment apparently devised and conducted, not by those in this world, but by those who have passed from this world into another mode of existence. It began significantly at the beginning of this century, shortly after the deaths of two of the most eminent pioneers in serious psychical research, Myers and Sidgwick, both of them classical scholars, and the cross-correspondence is loaded with classical excerpts and allusions and has come through several mediums. The experiment is far too long and complicated to be described in greater detail here, nor has it yet been fully assessed; but, so far as it has been collated, it is to be found in the Proceedings of the Society for Psychical Research. So also is an intriguing and similar type of case concerning Arthur, Lord Balfour, and the lady on whom he had set his affections. It is known as the Palm Sunday Case (*Proceedings of the SPR*, vol. 52, part 189). It would be going too far to say that cross-correspondence has established the identity of the communicators; but it is difficult to avoid the conclusion that some outside intelligences have been at work in an endeavour to prove to us their existence, and that these intelligences are aware of the sort of evidence which we require and of our difficulties in getting it; and there is a strong inference that these communicating intelligences are in fact what (or who) they purport to be.

It is not only at private séances that mediums operate. It has become a regular feature at services in many a spiritualist church for a medium to give a public demonstration of clairvoyance. These do not usually carry much conviction to the sceptic, though sometimes they are impressive, and they often seem to give great satisfactions to convinced spiritualists.

Sometimes mediums, especially those employing the technique of automatic writing, operate alone, and the scripts which they produce can be very interesting both to the psychical researcher and to the psychologist (e.g. *Swan on a Black Sea*, by Geraldine Cummins, Routledge and Kegan Paul). Sometimes mediums are called in to try to identify and locate a ghost or some other type of haunting or alleged case of possession. Sometimes they have been enlisted to unravel a crime or other mystery. Perhaps the term *medium* is in such cases misleading; but in such cases they are obviously exercising the *psi* faculty which every true medium must possess.

One way of triggering-off the *psi* faculty is by means of psychometry. This consists in giving the medium some article to hold as a result of which she appears the more easily to get in touch with the person with whom the article is associated or to acquire information concerning the article, such as the persons to whom it has belonged and the place from which it has come. Why this should happen is a mystery; but it nevertheless often appears to be the case. I will give one example from my own experience, for it enables me to mention one of the most remarkable mediums of recent times, the late Mrs Hester Dowden, and to describe an actual sitting with her.

⊂She was a very cultured gentlewoman, the daughter of the late Professor Dowden of Trinity College, Dublin. She married a Dr Travers-Smith, from whom she later separated, and sometimes she was known as Mrs Travers-Smith and sometimes as Mrs Dowden. She was very musical and fond of the theatre and she lived in a delightfully furnished house in Chelsea. Her *psi* faculties developed quite early and it was not till late in life that she eked out her income by becoming a professional medium. If one had a sitting with her, it took place in broad daylight in her spacious sitting-room. She did not appear to go into trance. She began her sittings by putting the ouija-board on her knees and inviting the sitter to join her in putting his fingers lightly on the pointer. As soon as this was done, the pointer would begin to move at a rapid pace and spell out a message. Mrs Dowden would then reverse the board and use it as a table on her knees, place on it some foolscap paper, pick up a pencil and begin automatic writing. She purported to be controlled by a guide called Johannes, and she veered between believing that Johannes really existed and thinking that he was probably a dramatised figment of her imagination. Once Johannes had come through, he would seek to introduce the deceased person (so far unnamed) whom the sitter wished to interview. It was at this point that Mrs Dowden liked to use psychometry to the limited extent of holding in her hand some object connected with the deceased. If the deceased did apparently come through, the sitter would ask questions to which the deceased appeared to reply by writing through the hand of Mrs Dowden. The handwriting did not vary according to who the communicator was, and the success or otherwise of the sitting consisted solely in the content of what was written. Success with Mrs Dowden was frequent and great. She herself took a lively interest in what her hand was writing and she would keep up a running commentary of intelligent remarks on what was happening.

One day, during a sitting, I wanted to give Mrs Dowden a test and, feeling rather at a loss as to what to do, I pulled out a gold fob and gave it to her to hold.

The effect was electric. For the one and only time in her life, so far as I know, Mrs Dowden exhibited a physical manifestation. Her hand began to shake and she called out, either to the communicator or to Johannes, 'Don't press so! You will break the point of the pencil.' I asked out loud who was there, and Mrs Dowden wrote the answer with a shaking hand and apparently with some difficulty. She wrote both the Christian name and the surname and she got them both right, despite the fact that names tend to come through badly. To me the whole episode was very interesting. The fob had belonged to the young man whose two names Mrs Dowden had written. He had died of tuberculosis in his late twenties some few years previously, quite unknown to the world at large and before ever I had met Mrs Dowden. He had been afflicted with some nervous complaint which had caused his hand to shake, so much so that he had had a specially strong nib put into his fountain-pen so that he should not break the point. He and I had been close friends from infancy and, on his death, his brother had given me this fob.

This little story illustrates what can happen at a successful sitting. It also raises some of the questions which are as yet unanswered. There can be no reasonable doubt as to Mrs Dowden's *psi* faculty. But did the deceased really come through? Or did Mrs Dowden gain the right information about him from my mind? In either case, why should she on this isolated occasion have been subjected to a physical manifestation? If she gained the information from the mind of the sitter, why should she appear to get it from the deceased? Did Johannes really exist, or was he merely a symbol with which Mrs Dowden's subconscious veiled her direct and psychic apprehension? Or are all such performances, as some claim, a satanic trick to deceive us, and, if so, with what object?

We are left guessing and each will decide for himself where the probabilities lie. (One possible reason for satanic activity is suggested in the last chapter.) The answer, however, will probably not be vouchsafed until we know much more about the *psi* faculty, and to know more, we must take into account all its many manifestations.

5

APPARITIONS, HAUNTINGS
AND POLTERGEISTS

APPARITIONS, ghosts and hauntings are of many kinds.
They are both of the living and the dead. They sometimes appear solid and sometimes insubstantial. They are
sometimes noisy and sometimes silent; sometimes pur-
poseful and sometimes seemingly meaningless; sometimes
aware of us and sometimes apparently unaware; sometimes benevolent and sometimes malicious, though more
often simply harmless. They may have the appearance of
humans or of animals or of inanimate objects or of
something for which we have no name. They may
exhibit a combination of two or more of these characteristics. In short, they seem to be as varied as the things
we meet in what we call the 'real' world. To this varied
list two phenomena must be added, the vision, usually
associated with a religious experience, and the poltergeist, which perhaps provides the most common of all
supernormal experiences. How much all these have in
common, apart from being as yet unexplained, is still a
matter for speculation. Ghost-stories of one sort or another
are common to all parts of the world and to all periods
of history, one of the earliest recorded ones being found
in Pliny's letters (Ep. VII, 27), while it would seem that
the author of the *Book of Job* knew something about

ghosts when he wrote, 'Fear came upon me and trembling, which made all my bones to shake. Then a spirit passed before my face; the hair of my flesh stood up' (Job 4. 14, 15). While making every allowance for dramatic exaggeration and distortion, it is difficult to believe that all these tales are without a substratum of fact, while some of the modern ones are very well authenticated.

We do not know how many ghosts there are or whether we have seen them. It is only when what we have seen disappears that we realise that it was an apparition.

The small boy, whose story is told in Chapter 1, was relating an experience which can be capped by many others.

Another boy whom I was interviewing in connection with some poltergeist-activities said that he had several times seen a ghost sitting in the chair which I was then occupying, and, he added, 'I'm scared.' Hoping to re-assure him, I said, 'There's no need for that. He hasn't tried to do you any harm. You're not frightened of me, are you?' 'No', said the boy, 'but you don't disappear.'

An undergraduate at Cambridge, coming home at about two o'clock in the morning, was walking behind an old man about twenty yards ahead, when the old man disappeared in the middle of Silver Street Bridge. The undergraduate did not wish to tell anyone in authority in his own College about this, because he was in breach of College rules by being out without a late leave, and the event took place at a time when discipline in the University was far more strict than it is today; but he was sufficiently impressed by his experience to go the next day to another College to report the incident to the late Professor Stratton, the astronomer and one-time President of the Society for Psychical Research.

In 1963 I was giving a course of lectures at a theological college, when one day the Principal told me that one of his students had, a day or so previously, seen a ghost. I was introduced to the student who took me up to his room and told me the following story. He was writing an essay one night after most of the House had gone to bed (they go early in theological colleges), when at about 11.30 he broke off work, got his toothbrush and, starting to brush his teeth as he went, left his room to make his way to the bathroom. Outside on the landing, only a few yards away underneath a lighted lamp was someone in a soutane. For a moment the student thought that it was another member of the College, but then saw that it was someone he did not know. For another moment he thought that it must be some clerical visitor who had lost his way. Then it occurred to him that it might be an apparition, and, as soon as this thought crossed his mind (but not before), the figure disappeared. Unperturbed, the student passed the spot where the figure had been standing and started his ablutions. While doing so, he was pondering the experience and he thought to himself, 'Ought I to be frightened?' and found that he was. He then rushed back to his own room, and jumped into bed and pulled the bedclothes over his head. Eventually he went to sleep and, in the morning, reported the incident to the Principal. The student says that he saw the apparition's face quite clearly and (for what it was worth) the Principal said that the description tallied with that of a former (and saintly) Principal. Perhaps it should be added that the student gave the impression of being a solid, down-to-earth Northerner and not the sort given to flights of fancy.

It will be noted that in two of the cases the apparition appeared solid and 'real' and was thought by the viewer to be an ordinary person until it disappeared. In the third case the apparition also appeared solid and real, but its disappearance took place *after* the student had, for some reason which he could not explain, doubted its 'reality'.

It will also be noted that, as in most casses where a ghost is seen, the ghost was in each instance clothed. In other words, the ghost in such cases is not merely the ghost of a person, it is also the ghost of inanimate objects, namely, the clothing. This has some bearing upon the nature of such apparitions, for, whatever they are, they cannot be simply the spirit of a departed person somehow made visible.

But not all apparitions bear the resemblance of the human form. Some are difficult to describe.

Two young men, aged about 17 to 20, were cleaning a church in Cambridge one bright morning. Suddenly one of them looked up and saw what he described as a ball of mist, a little bigger than a football, floating down the nave and turning left at the end. At that point he lost sight of it; but his companion, who had not till then seen anything unusual, picked up the view of it and saw it float towards the pulpit and disappear.

This story accords closely with one related of the Tower of London in the nineteenth century. In the home of one of the Yeoman Warders a party was sitting down to dinner one evening, when a ball of mist was seen to make the circuit of the table above the heads of those sitting at it and then disappear.

There is nothing in any of these cases just related to show whether the apparition was or was not a conscious entity. There are plenty of cases where the indications are that the apparitions are not conscious entities. One of these is related of a country rectory. It is not itself well authenticated, but it is typical of many a well-authenticated ghost-story.

From time to time a young woman in eighteenth-century dress is seen to climb out of a first-floor window, descend by a ladder, run across the garden and get into a coach, complete with driver and horses, and go off. Naturally, the popular local explanation is that she was eloping. It is to be noted that the total apparition consists of several ghosts. There is the ghost of the young woman, together with her clothing; there is the ghost of the coachman, with his clothing; there are the ghosts of the horses; and there are the ghosts of the ladder and the coach. The episode, furthermore, is recurrent, that is to say, very much the same story is related by a number of different persons who, on different occasions, claim to have seen the same sequence of events.

Cases of this sort seem to have something in common with the repeated running-through of a cinematograph film. The same actions are observed again and again; the characters are supported by the same theatrical props (clothes, ladder, coach and horses); but the actors do not seem to have any awareness of the presence of the percipients. It is tempting to conclude that in such cases something, at present unknown, has triggered off in the percipients some postcognitive faculty. The precognitive faculty enables the percipient to see into the future (see Chapter 3); the postcognitive factor enables him to see into the past. For that matter, some apparitions may possibly be explained by precognition—by the explanation that the percipient is seeing someone who is going to be at that spot in the future. But it is not all recurrent appearances that can be comfortably explained as postcognitive or precognitive experiences. In some recurrent cases, although the apparition seems to go through the same motions again and again, it also seems to take account of varying factors in what, to us, is the present and to adapt its behaviour accordingly.

One of the better authenticated cases of haunting is the *Morton Case*.[1] The apparition of a woman was seen by a number of persons over several years; at first appearing sufficiently solid to be mistaken for a living person, but gradually fading over the years. The apparition had no difficulty in negotiating threads stretched across the stairs. It did so by the simple expedient of ignoring them and passing through them, or, perhaps one should say, by causing them to pass through it. But, whenever anyone made an attempt to corner the apparition, it did not pass through its assailant, but took successful evasive action. This seems to indicate that, although the apparition was repetitive in its actions, it possessed an intelligence and an awareness of the solid, contemporary world. Such cases, therefore, suggest the presence of an intelligent entity, attracted to, or tied to, a particular locality, with some awareness of what is going on in our dimension, but not very interested by anything except its own affairs. These are thought by some to be 'earthbound spirits' of departed persons who do not know that they are dead, and stories are told of mediums who have made contact with them and re-leased them by convincing them of their true status. This may indeed sometimes be the case; but, if so, the *Morton* apparition may not be one of them. The fact that, over the years, the apparition grew less and less solid in appearance is more suggestive of the cinematograph-film type of explanation, with the film growing dimmer with age, though this in turn is contradicted by its apparent awareness of our conditions, evidenced by its taking evasive action.

Two of the most remarkable cases, probably of the cinematograph type, are the cases of Versailles and Dieppe. In the first, two Englishwomen visiting Versailles in 1901 seemed to be transported back to the Versailles of the eighteenth century[2] and, for a matter of hours, to be surrounded by the persons and architecture of that period. In the second, two Englishwomen visiting France near Dieppe (*Journal of the SPR* (1952) vol. XXXVI, No. 670, p. 607, and vol. 45, p. 55, 1969) in 1951 for a whole night heard the sound of explosions, as though the battle of the Second World War was being re-enacted.

Apparitions are not always of the dead; they are sometimes of the living (see *Phantasms of the Living* by E. Gurney). These apparitions often appear at times of crises, sometimes shortly before death. Sometimes they appear shortly after death or at the moment of death, when they cannot be classified as apparitions of the living, though otherwise the three types have much in common. It is difficult to distinguish those due to telepathy or to clairvoyance from those which are an actual visitation by the spirit of the person seen—of the person or animal, for apparitions of animals are also known. But they are not all associated with a crisis.

One of the more interesting and important cases is known as the *Wilmot case* and concerns a man and his wife (see *Proceedings of the SPR*, vol. VII, p. 41, and vol. XLVIII, p. 81). The couple had decided to emigrate and the wife had preceded her husband. The incident occurred while he was travelling to join her. The incident sharing a cabin with another man aboard a ship which was in the middle of the ocean. One night he saw his wife standing at the entrance to the cabin. He saw her hesitate and then come across the cabin and kiss him and disappear. He thought that his companion was asleep; but in fact the companion also saw the apparition and, although at the time he kept quiet, the next day he chaffed his cabin-mate about receiving women in the cabin in the middle of the night. But what makes the case so important is that it is one of those where the person viewed had the reciprocal experience to that of the viewer, that is to say, the wife had the experience of seeing her husband lying in his bunk; she wanted to kiss him, but hesitated to intrude, because she saw also the other man in his bunk; but, although she hesitated, she determined to go on, and did so.

It may be that this case should be classified as one of the out-of-the-body experiences. But it may also be classified as an apparition of the living, and such cases are important in that they provide a clue about the question of survival. Professor Hornell Hart and a team of assistants have made a valuable comparison between cases reported of apparitions of the living and apparitions of the dead ('Six Theories about Apparitions', *Proceedings of the SPR*, vol. 50, p. 153). From the researcher's point of view, apparitions of the living are especially useful because it is possible to question not only the viewer, but also the person viewed. It has been found that the person viewed sometimes has an experience reciprocal to that of the viewer. This seems to prove that an apparition is sometimes an intelligent entity, knowing what it is doing and appreciating what is going on in the 'solid' world around it. A comparison of such cases with apparitions of the dead reveals that in many instances there are sufficient points of similarity to justify one in drawing the tentative conclusion that some apparitions of the dead are also intelligent entities, knowing what they are doing and appreciating what is going on in the 'solid' world around them. Although this conclusion can be only tentative, it goes some way towards strengthening the arguments in favour of survival.

A puzzling form of apparition, rare but known, is where the viewer sees an apparition of himself. Tyrrell 'Six Theories About Apparitions', *Proceedings of the SPR*, vol. 50, pp. 129 ff.) gives three such cases. In one of them a woman, in company with three other persons, saw an apparition of herself while they were having supper. Her three companions saw it too. An interesting feature of the case is that the apparition was wearing a dress which at that time the woman did not possess, but which, it subsequently transpired, was like one which two years later she did wear. This may be a case of precognition intruding once again but, on this occasion, a collective precognition. It may, however, be a rare case of an out-of-the-body experience (see Chapter 6).

Apparitions are usually spontaneous occurrences, but there are a few recorded instances of experiments which have successfully induced an apparition (see Gurney's *Phantasm of the Living* and Tyrrell's *Myers Memorial Lecture* for the SPR). The experimenter thinks hard of himself in some other place and, if the experiment is successful, someone sees him in that place. The apparition however, appears in such cases superficially to have a volition of its own independent of that of the experimenter, for it appears to go through motions very similar to those of spontaneous apparitions, and ones of which the experimenter is neither thinking nor aware. Such cases, therefore, differ from out-of-the-body experiences (see Chapter 6) and suggest that perhaps the viewer unconsciously plays a part in determining the details of the apparent manifestation. This is not altogether surprising, for we do a great deal of unconscious interpreting with everything we see or hear and it is the interpreted result which ultimately impinges on our consciousness. But, if this is what happens in the case of the experimentally induced apparition, there is no reason to suppose that it does not also happen in the spontaneous cases. It may be, therefore, that some of the features which puzzle us can be attributed to faulty interpretation.

In the popular mind, hauntings are mainly associated with visible manifestations of ghosts, yet it seems likely that there are many more cases of poltergeists. The word *poltergeist* is German and means 'noisy ghost'. More often than not a poltergeist is heard and not seen, the noises ranging from raps and footsteps to loud crashes and bangs. It also throws about solid objects sometimes at persons, but more often about the room. It often begins by moving small objects, such as ornaments, from one part of a room to another, doing so when no one is in the room. For a time the occupants of the house do not suspect poltergeist activity and are simply puzzled to explain why these small objects are so frequently turning up in the wrong place. Then the poltergeist becomes more bold and more effective and begins to throw ornaments about in the presence of the occupants. Sometimes it moves large pieces of furniture and piles such pieces on top of each other. Sometimes it communicates with the occupants by means of raps. The occupants will address the poltergeist and lay down a simple code, such as 'one rap for *yes* and two raps for *no*', and will then put questions to the poltergeist to which it replies by raps. All this may appear very improbable; but poltergeist activities are well authenticated and there are very many accounts of them to be found in the literature of psychical research.[3]

Among the records of the SPR is one unpublished

report which is particularly impressive in that it is a police-report, the police having been called in by an occupant who was ignorant of the existence of poltergeists and who was concerned about the disturbances in his house. This was a case in which large pieces of furniture were moved across the room in the presence of witnesses.

One poltergeist chose an unusual location for its manifestations. It chose a lorry. The lorry was being used by a party of English schoolboys, aged about sixteen and seventeen, who, with a couple of masters, travelled in it from England to Greece and back. On two separate occasions, while the lorry was parked in the countryside with its engine off, and while the party was on the ground nearby, the lorry was convulsed by violent shakings. There was no earthquake and all around was still, and the shakings were so violent that the combined party was unable subsequently to reproduce them with the lorry. These convulsions went on for about two minutes, and, on one occasion, they ceased, when a boy loudly invoked the Deity. No normal explanation was ever forthcoming and nothing peculiar in the history of the lorry was ever discovered. This account was recorded and deposited in the archives of the SPR.

No one knows what precisely a poltergeist is. It is thought by many to be a mischievous and low-grade entity of pure spirit, that is, something which is, and always has been, simply a spirit and is not the spirit of a deceased person. An angel is by definition a pure spirit who has never been a human; they are a different order of creation from humans, and (*pace* Victorian tombstones) humans do not become angels on quitting their human frame, though they leave the material world for the world of spirit to which angels belong. Since angels are reputedly good or bad, there seems no reason to suppose that some may be simply low-grade, perhaps more bad than good, but rather purposeless and ineffective, and, since poltergeist activities seem to be singularly purposeless and often rather ineffectual, it may be that those are right who regard poltergeist as low-grade spirits.

But there is another school of thought which attributes poltergeist activities to the unconscious actions of a human being, more often an adolescent. It is certainly true that these activities occur very frequently when there is an adolescent around. Adolescent girls are more often associated with them than adolescent boys. The manifestations have been known to cease when the adolescent is removed. They have been known to recur in the place to which the adolescent has gone. Adolescents have been strongly suspected of causing the activities by trickery. *Trickery* is perhaps a better word to use than *fraud*, both in this context and in the context of a physical medium who has been caught in the act; for in both cases the agent (the adolescent or the medium) may be at times perfectly genuine, producing genuine psychic phenomena, and producing them while in a state which is in some degree abnormal, and in the case of the physical medium, at times very abnormal, giving the impression of deep trance. On occasions there may be a strong desire, conscious or subconscious, to produce phenomena, and the phenomena may not come. It is then that the agent may succumb to the temptation to produce apparent psychic phenomena by trickery. But it may be a temptation to which, in a normal state the agent would not succumb. One must be cautious about attributing to a person in an abnormal state the same degree of responsibility as one might attribute to a person in a normal state. Admittedly, there are times when such charitable restraint seems scarcely credible; but there is yet another factor to take into account, and that is the possibility of possession, total or partial. Some mediums certainly appear to be possessed, when they go into deep trance, their bodies, brain, speaking mechanism and everything physical seeming to be taken over completely by another entity, usually their benevolent guide, but sometimes a deceased person with whom contact is being sought. In a case of complete possession, any trickery should presumably be attributed solely to the possessing entity; but in a case of partial possession, it is difficult to know who or what is responsible or to what extent.

There is, however, a third possibility concerning poltergeists and it is perhaps the most likely one. It is that the poltergeist needs to draw power from a human being before it can operate and that, for some reason unkown, it finds a source of power in an adolescent which is more easily tapped than that in a child or fully grown person. The donor whose power is being tapped is not conscious of the tapping operation, and may be as perturbed as others at the manifestations to which he or she is unwittingly contributing; but, when the donor is withdrawn, the manifestations cease for lack of power or sometimes are transferred to the donor's new locality.

The suggestion that a poltergeist draws power from a human being gains credibility when one remembers that at some séances raps are heard and tables are moved when a group of persons are deliberately seeking psychic phenomena. Sometimes the withdrawal of a single person from the group results in a weakening or cessation of the phenomena, while additions to the group result in an increase in manifestations in their strength.

But, if poltergeists sometimes, perhaps usually, draw their power from human beings in the vicinity, this is not always the case, for poltergeist activities have been known to occur in empty houses and to have been discovered on a subsequent visit only by the displacement of the furnishings. In any event, if a human being be in fact the source of the poltergeist's power, there does not always seem to be any need for the human to be in close proximity to the manifestations, since these occur sometimes in parts of the house where no one is about.

Mr G. W. Lambert has argued strongly (SPR *Journal*, vol. XXXVIII, pp. 49, 149, 201 and 276) for a theory that poltergeist activities are really due to the action of the tides in underground channels. The argument, to me, is unconvincing. Underground water might account for some of the noises heard, but not for many of the instances of the movement of furniture.

At times it seems that one type of psychic activity attracts another. An attempt to use the ouija-board may result in raps being heard in different parts of the room. A house which is haunted by a visible, but silent, ghost may also prove the focus for poltergeist activities which appear to be unconnected with the visible apparition. It is rash to generalise about these matters, but there is some ground for thinking that evil attracts evil. A harmless apparition may be associated with a locality in which no other manifestations occur; but a malevolent entity seems to attract other mischievous entities.

But, although evil may attract evil, any type of psychical phenomenon seems likely to attract other types. I will give two instances.

My family one summer occupied the home-farm on the estate of a relative. It was a Tudor building and had the reputation in the locality of being heavily haunted. During our brief occupancy of the place a number of odd events occurred, not very obviously connected with each other. Twice the household was awoken in the night by enormous rumblings in the roof. No normal explanation for this was ever discovered, though the house was repeatedly searched from top to bottom. These noises were well known and were attributed by the locals, very improbably, to the ghost of a smuggler rolling his barrels overhead. On several occasions loud clanking noises were heard in different rooms, coming apparently from immediately behind the head of the bed in each room when someone was in bed. One still afternoon, at about two o'clock, a grandfather clock (which had fairly recently been brought to the house) started to go and went for about two minutes, with its pendulum swinging, although the clock had never gone since it was bought, and, in fact, was without a key. For other accounts of the spontaneous starting of clockwork see SPR *Journal* 47 (December, 1974), pp. 479, 480.

In another house, also dating from Tudor times, though mainly Queen Anne, there was supposed to be a grey lady. Our predecessor in the house saw her one day in broad daylight. He came out of the door of a room on the ground floor and saw what he thought was a visitor coming towards him. He stood aside to let her pass. To his surprise she turned into a lobby in which coats were hung and which had no other entrance. He followed her in order to show her the way out and found that she had disappeared. My family never met her; but, upstairs, in a different part of the house, we sometimes saw a door open with no visible cause. The handle of the door was a typical Queen Anne drop-ring which one lifted and turned to open the door. The lock seemed to be in perfect order. When the door mysteriously opened, we would see the drop-ring lift and turn, as though manipulated by an invisible hand. So far as we could discover, there was no connection between this and the grey lady on the ground floor.

Certainly not all hauntings appear to be evil. In a house in a cathedral close there appear to be two unconnected ghosts. One is of a little dog and the other of an old woman. The then occupants of the house were careful not to talk about the ghosts in front of the young children of the household, until they discovered from a casual remark by one of the children that they knew all about the old woman. Far from being frightened, the children used to play with her and liked her.

Most cases of haunting seem to be innocuous, save for the fright which they engender. But there are cases where the haunting entity or entities are anything but harmless. Physical assaults on persons have been known to occur. Just as solid furniture appears not to be immune from physical interference by some non-physical entity, so a human is not immune from physical attack by a non-physical entity. Two such entities have come to be known as *incubi* and *succubi*. Reference is found to them many centuries ago. Both (if they exist, as they appear to do) are demons, the incubus assuming a male form and seeking to consort with women, the succubus assuming a female form (and, therefore, sometimes called a *succuba*) and seeking to consort with men.

One case of haunting, possibly due to an incubus or a succubus, but certainly involving physical assault, occurred to a woman in her mid-forties in a very old inn. The inn, unknown to the victim at the time, had a reputation for being heavily haunted, especially on a certain staircase and in one particular room. This room was assigned to the victim on her arrival. She had closed the door and began to unpack, when she felt a hand descend so heavily on her shoulder that she nearly lost her balance. Thinking that it was a chambermaid who had returned unnoticed to the room, she called out, 'Take care! You nearly knocked me over.' She then looked round and, to her astonishment, found the room empty and the door still closed. Two days later when she went to bed in the same room, she turned out the light at about 11.15 p.m. and got into bed. After the lapse of about three minutes, she suddenly felt the pressure of hands on either side of her, not actually on her body, but on the bedclothes on either side, drawing them tightly across her chest. She also felt hot breath on her face. She sat up, lit a match and exclaimed, 'Who is it? What do you want?' She saw and heard nothing; but she was not unnaturally frightened and said that she had a strong feeling of oppression. She got out of bed, turned on the light by the door, and thoroughly searched the room, but discovered nothing of significance. The feeling of oppression, however, suddenly lifted and she got her rosary, hung it around her neck, turned out the light and got back into bed. Being a woman of fortitude, she occupied the room for two more nights; but, being also circumspect, she refused to have it when, on a subsequent visit, it was allotted to her. This caused no surprise to the landlady, because other guests had apparently had unpleasant experiences in that room and subsequently it was withdrawn from commission as a bedroom.

In such cases as these, some malevolent influence appears to be at work and there is evidence to support the view that exorcism (see Chapter 10) is indicated and can be effective. But it must be emphasised that most hauntings do not threaten physical harm, though they can certainly be frightening and in some cases may result in spiritual harm, especially to those who ill-advisedly and from frivolous motives seek them out.

In addition to the ghostly apparition there is also the vision of the sort which saints down the ages have claimed to see. There are points in common between the holy vision and the ghostly apparition. They both come and go suddenly and they both tend to be insubstantial by our standards. Sometimes they speak and sometimes they are silent, and in both cases it is difficult to know how much is to be regarded as objective and how much is coloured by the interpretation of the viewer. The religious vision seems to clothe itself in the trappings which the viewer would expect. The visions in the Book of Daniel and in the Revelation of St. John the Divine, for example, are such as one might expect if one were a devout Jew of the period. Our Lady of Lourdes looked much as Bernadette might have imagined her to look. The same cannot be said of her speech, save that it was in the local dialect; but the content of the speech, as reported by the viewer, 'I am the Immaculate Conception'; must be one of the oddest modes of declaring an identity ever recorded.

But, whatever the type of the apparition, several questions present themselves.

How far are they subjective or objective? It seems possible that in some instances the viewer contributes a lot to his own experience, and to that extent apparitions may be termed subjective. But there must be *something* external to the viewer which triggers off his subjective experience, and to that extent an apparition is objective.

Is it material or immaterial? It seems capable of exhibiting both qualities. When apparitions pass through walls and furniture, they appear more immaterial than material. When they walk round a table, instead of through it, or take steps to evade attempts to touch them, they are behaving as though they are material. The poltergeist is usually invisible; but its capacity to make a noise and to throw things about indicates that it is, in part at least, material; and the incubus and succubus are unpleasantly material in so far as their victims feel them, but immaterial in so far as they are invisible.

We are clearly dealing with a range of phenomena which, being unlike anything within our normal experience, we have not learnt to measure or evaluate. Attempts have been made to photograph ghosts so as to ascertain whether the camera sees what the human eye appears to see. But, although some success is claimed, the evidence is not very convincing. More satisfactory is the evidence of the thermometer. This has frequently registered a marked drop in temperature when ghostly phenomena are occurring. The mirror also has, within its limits, confirmed the impression of the viewer by displaying a reflection of an apparition (see Tyrrell's *Myers Memorial Lecture*, p. 63).

But the true nature of an apparition has so far eluded us, partly, perhaps, because there are many different causes operating to bring about phenomena which superficially have similar appearances, but in fact are fundamentally different.

6

OUT-OF-THE-BODY EXPERIENCES

WHEN a person leaves his body for a time and then returns to it with a recollection of what has occurred, away from the body he is said to have had an out-of-body experience. Claims to have had this experience may be very difficult to refute or to substantiate. It implies that the body is something separable from the essential personality, rather than an integral part of the total personality. This, of course, is implied whenever we talk of survival of bodily death. We mean that our bodies are dispensable in the same way that our toe-nails or our teeth or our hair are dispensable. While they are with us, they contribute to our totality; but we can part with them without serious detriment to our totality, and, after they are gone, the important part of us still remains. But, be that as it may, we know what the speaker is seeking to convey, when he says that he has left his body, and we are more concerned about the truth or falsity of the statement. Assuming that the speaker is honest, has he had a veridical experience or a mere fantasy?

Often it is difficult to judge. But it is rash to deny the possibility of such an experience. So many persons claim to have had it and there runs through so many of their accounts a striking thread of similarity. The stories may perhaps be conveniently categorised under two main headings, the spontaneous and the induced.

In the spontaneous cases, the person having the experience typically describes how, when in a recumbent position, he suddenly finds himself floating above his ordinary body which he can see lying some feet beneath him. As often as not he describes how his floating self appears to be attached to his recumbent self by a tenuous cord or cable. This seems to have the property of infinite extension, for the floating self sometimes goes off on a voyage of exploration, being apparently able to propel itself to any desired destination by the mere act of thinking about that destination. The mind of the person seems to be located in the floating body, the recumbent body being inert and seemingly mindless. Eventually the traveller decides to return, sometimes with reluctance and hesitation, sometimes with some degree of panic, whereupon the floating self descends into the recumbent self, usually gently, but sometimes with a 'plop', and normality is resumed. The memory of the experience, however, remains; at least, it does so in the recorded cases, though one is left to speculate whether the experience may be more common without leaving any trace on the memory and therefore, never recorded. One is also left to speculate as to *how* a memory of the experience is registered, since awareness appears to reside in the floating or disembodied self; rather than in the recumbent self which, however, still retains all the solid matter of the body, including the mechanism of the brain for registering experiences and recording them for future reference. Indeed, speculation along these lines leads to further speculation about the very nature of mind. The brain is matter; mind is an activity and is usually regarded as an activity of the brain. Assuming that we have souls, does the brain pass information to the soul through the mind? Or does the soul pass ideas to the brain through the mind? Or is it a two-way traffic, the brain instructing the soul and the soul activating the brain, the mind being the flow of messages in each direction? If the floating self can gain experiences which the recumbent self can register as memory, it presumably does so through the soul which both selves share.

The tenuous cord or cable attaching the floating body to the recumbent body has great importance attributed to it, and it is said that, so long as it remains intact, the person is alive, but that, if it snaps, death has supervened. It is claimed that this is the 'silver cord' in the passage, 'Or ever the silver cord be loosed, or the golden bowl be broken, or the pitcher be broken at the fountain, or the wheel broken at the cistern. Then shall the dust return to the earth as it was: and the spirit shall return unto God who gave it.[1]

The induced experiences are similar to the spontaneous ones, save that the agency inducing them is more obvious. Persons have described very similar experiences while anaesthetised and apparently profoundly unconscious and undergoing a surgical operation. Such experiences have also been described by persons who have been rendered unconscious in an accident. Their descriptions include the experience of looking down on the recumbent body and also of being aware of their loose attachment to it by the silver cord.

Many of these accounts are, in isolation, evidentially unsatisfactory in that they depend solely on the evidence of the person claiming to have had the experience. To relate such an experience is to put one's veracity in issue; but, further, even if one's veracity be not impugned, there still remains the question of whether the experience was veridical or mere fantasy. One person I know was anaesthetised in order to undergo the extraction of a tooth. His own account of the matter was that he remained fully conscious, though at no time suffering pain, and with his eyes closed, and that he heard a conversation between the dentist and the anaesthetist of a sort which a patient would not be permitted to hear, concerning a difficulty which the dentist was experiencing in the course of the operation. When he was fully awake again, he delightedly recounted to the dentist and the anaesthetist what he believed had taken place, only to be assured by them that nothing of the sort had occurred, that he had clearly been fully anaesthetised, that they had encountered no difficulty in performing the operation, and that, in short, his alleged experience was pure fantasy. He accepted their assurance, but only with difficulty, for the experience had been to him very convincing. This story is a warning against too ready an acceptance as veridical of an experience which rests solely on the belief of the person relating it.

But there are accounts of out-of-the-body experiences which do not rest solely on the testimony of the person who claims to have had the experience. Dr Robert Crookall has written extensively on the subject.[2] One of the cases cited by him relates how a woman had the experience due to asphyxiation by a defective gas-jet in an hotel where she was staying. Out of the body she travelled to her home and her husband's bedroom, and saw there another man asleep as well as her husband and, leaning against the bed, a cudgel. She then returned to her body and, after a period of unconsciousness, she was revived, having very nearly died. Subsequent investigation disclosed that there really had been a second man sleeping in her husband's bedroom that night and that there really had been a cudgel such as she described.

That is one type of verification, the collection by the

'traveller' of information concerning the place visited. If the information is such that the traveller would not normally have known it, there is some corroboration of the traveller's account of an out-of-the-body visit to the location. It can be conclusive evidence of the traveller's psychic sensitivity; but it is not in itself conclusive proof that an out-of-the-body journey has been taken. It could, for example, be a case of clairvoyance, rationalised by the sensitive as a case of travelling. There are, however, other indications that the probable explanation is that given by the traveller, namely, that he has been out of the body on what is sometimes called an astral journey.

One such indication is provided when the traveller, as well as seeing, is also seen. This by no means always occurs. For example, although there are many cases where a patient, under an anaesthetic and in the operating theatre, claims to have floated above his body and watched the performance of the operation, I know of no case where the persons engaged on the performance of the operation have seen anything of significance other than the physical body of the patient on the operating table. Dr Crookall[3] gives a number of instances where a person has been seen while in fact his body has been elsewhere. They are not strictly cases of out-of-the-body experiences, because in none of the instances which he cites was the person seen aware of having travelled. Out-of-the-body experiences are sometimes called *astral projections*, and the cases cited by Dr Crookall may be so termed, even though the person seen was unaware of having made a journey. In one such case a man, anxious about his wife who was away and ill in hospital, was seen by the night-nurse who reported to the sister that someone was prowling about the building. When, the next day, he did visit the hospital, this nurse, as soon as she saw him, accused him of being the man she had seen. At the time that she thought that she had seen him he was certainly thinking about the hospital; but he had no experience of actually visiting it. This type of case (and there are many like it) is more akin to the deliberately induced apparition.[4] In a true out-of-the-body experience, the traveller has, in some form, actually been to a place while leaving his physical body elsewhere. But in these other cases he has merely thought about that place and his thought has somehow created something which has become visible at that place without his having the the experience of being there. It may be some sort of astral projection (one may coin words and phrases as one pleases to denote these unusual events); but what has been created is a thought-form with, apparently, some volition of its own.

The claims of those who say that they have had out-of-the-body experiences are further corroborated to some extent by some death-bed phenomena. There are on record instances where the by-standers say that, shortly before death, they have seen a second body rising in a misty form from the recumbent body of the patient. They say, moreover, that the two bodies are joined together by a silver cord. There comes a point in time, they say, when the cord snaps and the second body disappears and the recumbent body dies.

Some who say that they have had an out-of-the-body experience also claim that they have had a preview of the hereafter, or, rather, of the immediate hereafter. But, in the nature of things, such claims can be neither verified nor refuted.

A whole body of theory has grown up round these out-of-the-body experiences. It would certainly seem that we may have at least two bodies, the physical, which remains where we expect it to be, and the 'astral' which can sometimes leave the physical and go off on a journey on its own. But some theories go further than that and state that we have a whole series of bodies, which peel off like onion-skins and mark different stages of our progress, first here, and then in different *strata* of the hereafter. This theory, in one form or another, is very old and belief in the possession by us of more than one body is widespread. It finds its place in Anglican theology. The Order for the Burial of the Dead in the Book of Common Prayer incorporates that difficult and disputed passage from the Book of Job which in the Authorised Version runs, ' . . . though after my skin worms destroy this body, yet in my flesh shall I see God',[5] and the thought is picked up by St Paul in another passage incorporated into the Burial Service[6] where he writes, 'How are the dead raised up? And with what body do they come? . . . That which thou sowest is not quickened, except it die . . . Thou sowest not that body which shall be, but bare grain . . . But God giveth it a body . . . There are also celestial bodies, and bodies ter-restrial . . . There is a natural body, and there is a spiritual body.' However many bodies there may be, the existence of only a second body, capable of operating away from the physical body, gives support to the view that there is survival after death in that it tends to prove that the purely physical is not the whole of us, and that, therefore, we do not necessarily come to an end with the dissolution of the physical body.

7

HYPNOTISM

HYPNOTISM is a fringe subject, bestriding the borders of orthodox medicine and psychical research and finding a place also (and undesirably) in the repertoire of music-hall performances. In one form or another it has been practised down the ages and in every part of the world. In the West, however, it received its greatest impetus from Dr Mesmer towards the end of the eighteenth-century and the beginning of the nineteenth century. As a result of his activities it was for a time known as *Mesmerism* and the word still survives.

Dr Mesmer was a colourful personality. He was an Austrian physician, who made his name in Paris in about 1775. He was not a quack, but he was for a time thought to be so, and he aroused the hostility of more orthodox practitioners in medicine. That is not a difficult feat to accomplish and Mesmer's conduct provided grounds for suspicion of him. He dabbled in astrology and treated his patients in a dramatic way, being himself clothed in esoteric garments. At first he believed that his therapeutic agency was a form of electricity which flowed from his hands and into his patients or from magnets with which he made passes over the patients, and he also believed in similar emanations flowing from the planets. But later he abandoned this theory and believed instead that an invisible fluid emanated from his hands and into his patients.

However erroneous his theories may have been, his practice worked. It was almost certainly a form of what we now call hypnotism, depending for its success on the suggestibility of the patient and the skill of the practitioner in inducing and using this suggestibility. Since, however, there is still a lot to be discovered about hypnotism, and since what looks like hypnotism may in fact be more than one thing, it is as well to keep in the back of one's mind the faint possibility that there may be some foundation in fact for Mesmer's theory concerning emanations from the hands. That the body exudes some insubstantial substance is a very widely held belief, particularly among those who claim to see auras around the body.[1]

One of the most useful properties of hypnotism is that it can produce anaesthesia. For this reason, in the first half of the nineteenth century, after Mesmer, it was taken up by the medical profession and might have developed sooner and further than has in fact been the case, had it not been for the discovery of anaesthetics. In India a whole hospital was established for surgical cases, where all the operations were performed on patients who were anaesthetised solely by hypnotism.

Its effects can be very striking: I have myself witnessed tooth extractions from patients who have been anaesthetised solely by hypnotism. Sometimes they were wholly anaesthetised hypnotically and sometimes they were given a local (hypnotic) anaesthetic when only a single tooth was to be extracted. The process was not speedy; but it was effective. The suggestions given to the patients were that they should co-operate with the dentist by doing such things as opening the mouth wider, rinsing it out, and the like; that they would feel no pain; that there would be no bleeding; that afterwards they would feel happy and well; and sometimes the additional suggestion was given that they would have no recollection of the operation from the moment that they went under until the moment when, at the command of the hypnotist, they came out of the hypnotic trance. The suggestions worked. One woman had seven extractions (to be accurate, six and a half, since one tooth broke); each tooth came out bloody, but within thirty seconds of the last extraction we were inspecting her mouth and there was no bleeding visible. She woke up laughing and jumped off the platform and, half an hour later, was eating a solid and hearty meal with the rest of us.

But, in addition to anaesthesia, many other effects can be obtained under hypnotism. The patient can be made to go so rigid that his head can be placed on one chair and his heels on another so that he forms a bridge between the two, of such strength that it will support the weight of two or three persons sitting on him. It can be successfully suggested to him that he will neither see nor hear a particular person or object within his field of vision. He can be induced to perform a whole range of actions, though it is claimed that he cannot be induced to perform one which runs counter to his moral principles. If, for instance, he is told to stab someone, he may go through the motions of stabbing, but, it is suggested, will stop short of the actual performance. He can, moreover, be given a post-hypnotic suggestion. He may, for example, be told that precisely 31 minutes after being called out of trance he will, for no reason, go to another room and return with a candlestick, or that at half-past two the next afternoon he will telephone someone. Not only may these post-hypnotic suggestions be successful, but the patient may exhibit an astonishing accuracy in the timing of his performance.

Apart from such interesting experiments as these, hypnotism has been put to various uses. Anaesthesia has already been mentioned. It has been used also for the removal of the symptoms of various diseases, especially the removal of pain and discomfort; though, clearly, this is not to be generally recommended, since symptoms are of value both diagnostically and as a warning. Hypnotism has also been used to remove anxiety, for example before an examination, or to induce a good night's rest, and even to encourage memory. Diagnostically it has sometimes been used by psychiatrists to uncover a traumatic experience which the patient has relegated to the subconscious.

Whereas Mesmer, to induce hypnotism, experimented at first by passing magnets close to the body of the patient, but later made passes with the hand alone, today hypnotism is regarded as the product of suggestion and is usually induced by suggestion alone. The patient reclines comfortably in a chair and sometimes he is made to look at some small object, such as a ring, held by the hypnotist in such a position that to look at it is a slight strain on the patient's eyes. He is then told that his eyes are getting tired, which first suggestion, being true, he accepts. He is next told to close his eyes, which first command he readily obeys, because that is what he feels like doing. Having been thus introduced to a mood of acquiescence he is next subjected to further commands and suggestions, delivered firmly, but soothingly, until, in a successful case, complete acceptance of suggestions and commands is induced and continues until such time as the hypnotist by a command awakes the patient, usually leaving him with the final suggestion that he is now quite free of the hypnotist's influence and of the effects of the hypnotism.

There is much about hypnotism which is still unknown; but its phenomena and claims are as firmly established as anything could be. What, it may be asked, has it to do with psychical research? Quite a lot, though no one knows precisely how much. If one takes Mesmer as one's starting-point, hypnotism started as an excursion into the unknown of a sort which would have attracted psychical researchers, if there had then been any psychical researchers to attract. It was pursued in the face of disapproval by the incredulous and the orthodox, and it won its way only by the manifest proof of the truth of its claims coupled with its utilitarian value therapeutically and anaesthetically. The first explanation of its mechanics, namely, that it was induced electrically, was erroneous; and the second explanation, of the mesmeric fluid, was probably also erroneous. But the *fact* of hypnotism remained, together with its extraordinary manifestations, still largely unexplained. In all this it bears a close resemblance to much else in psychical research. But its relevance to that study is closer still.

It looks very much as though the medium who goes into trance does so by the mechanics of self-hypnotism. Hypnotism by itself does not produce psychic phenomena, but it looks as though it is one of the means by which a psychically endowed person can switch out of the normal wavelength and onto the psychic wavelength.

In one type of psychic experiment hypnotism is deliberately used. It is called *sending a person travelling* and it bears so close a resemblance to out-of-the-body experiences that it may be regarded as an induced form of such experiences in contrast to the more usual spontaneous experiences. In these experiments, a suitable subject is hypnotised and remains physically in the same place, but is told to go in spirit or in thought to some other place and then come back and report on what he has discovered there. If his report accords with the facts, the experiment is successful. In one such case, reported by Myers,[2] the traveller was told to visit a certain house (in mind or spirit) to which she had never been and report what she found there. She reported that there was a grotesque and very corpulent person sitting by a table, neither eating nor drinking. This description was not in the least what the experimenter was expecting, and he thought that the experiment had been a failure. But it transpired afterwards that the person charged with setting the scene and who the experimenter had thought would remain there had instead gone out, but had first caused a dummy to be made up to look like a person, with an extra pillow inserted into the clothes to make the dummy appear fat. This was done entirely without the knowledge of the experimenter who had ordered the traveller to visit this house.

There is no reason to suppose that, under hypnotism, anyone chosen at random can be sent travelling. It is more probable that the experiment will be successful only with a person who has a latent psychic faculty. It may be, of course, that we all have the latent faculty; but, if that be so, it is probably stronger, or at least nearer the surface, in some than it is in others. Hypnotism is clearly a potent factor in bringing about changes in the working of the body. It can inhibit pain; it can remove psychological inhibitions; it can affect the control of our bodily mechanism in areas over which we normally have little control, such as the adrenalin secretions which themselves affect our tendencies to bleed; and it can give us hallucinations so that we think that something is present which is not present or that something is not present which is present. It may be that with a person with a strong psychic faculty hypnotism inhibits the normal mechanism of mind and body, leaving the abnormal, psychic faculty a free field in which to play. The other side of the picture, however, is that hypnotism demonstrates how vulnerable we are to suggestion, and this should make us more wary about accepting at face-value accounts of marvels, in that, though they may be given in good faith, they may nevertheless be coloured by the suggestibility of our own imaginations.

8

VARIETIES OF ESP

AS has been said, it may be that everyone is possessed of the *psi* faculty, though undoubtedly it is stronger in some than in others. It would seem that in any given person an increase in sophistication can lead to a decrease in the *psi* faculty. This is by no means always so. No one would dub Gilbert Murray as unsophisticated, and anyone who knew Mrs Hester Dowden would agree that she was a highly cultured and sophisticated woman, and yet in both the *psi* faculty was manifest in a high degree. But, although there are no statistics on the point, it does look as though an increase in sophistication often leads to a decrease in the *psi* faculty and that each is to some extent a compensation for deficiency in the other. Just as a blind person may have an increased acuity of hearing to compensate for the absence of sight, so a person without the aids which sophistication brings may have a compensating ESP. One can but guess; but animals often appear to have a more acute ESP than human beings. They seem to be as much aware of a psychic presence, such as an apparition, as are humans, and they give the same indication of awareness on occasions when humans have sensed nothing. Peoples in the less developed parts of the world seem to be endued with the *psi* faculty far more frequently and far more strongly than peoples in the developed countries. It is impossible to be in West Africa, for example, for any length of time without becoming aware of the extent to which ju-ju (as it is called) dominates the lives of the inhabitants. Ju-ju, sometimes called witchcraft, may perhaps be better described as the practice and awareness of the occult. It is easy to dismiss it as baseless superstition; but that is seldom the attitude of Europeans who have actually lived in the area and seen it at work. One of its manifestations is an awareness of events which have happened far away before the sophisticated means of communication have had the opportunity to operate. In the Western world children, too, often seem to have a *psi* faculty in infancy which declines as they grow older. Anyone in Germany who has watched the very young children of members of the British Forces stationed there playing with the equally young German children will have been impressed by the *rapport* and understanding between them despite the absence of a common language. They not only seem to understand each other with ease, but they are also quick to interpret to their respective adults the needs and wishes of their foreign playmates.

The *psi* faculty manifests itself in a number of different ways, some of which have already been mentioned. But, since those that have been mentioned by no means exhaust the list, it is as well to look briefly at some of the others and also to touch on practices and beliefs which are common, though not necessarily well founded.

Psychometry has been mentioned[1] in connection with mediumship; but it is not confined to mediumship. Many a sensitive who is not a medium appears to get information by holding an object, such as a watch or a ring or a pen, in the hand. The information may be about the history of the object held, or about the owner or about former owners. It has been used to discover the whereabouts of missing persons and is claimed to have led sometimes to the discovery of a body or of a murderer. Without passing judgement on some of these more dramatic claims, there is no doubt that at times psychometry works. How it works is a different matter. There are those who believe that the object is somehow impregnated with influences from past associations. This seems very doubtful, especially when one observes that the sensitive using psychometry is eclectic in the information obtained, tending to give only the information relevant to the immediate purpose of the inquiry. It is more probable that the object has no intrinsic psychic virtue, but that it acts as a catalyst enabling the sensitive to switch on the psychic faculty, and thereby obtain by ESP the desired information.

Fortune-telling, whether by palmistry, playing-cards, tea-leaves, or some other means, is an ancient and widespread pastime. The expression includes character-reading and a reading of the past history of the person concerned, as well as a foretelling of what is in store for him. The practitioners claim to get their results by observing the lines on the palm of the hand, or by the playing-cards which are turned up, or by the pattern of tea-leaves left in the dregs at the bottom of a cup. It is often manifest nonsense; but sometimes one meets a practitioner who gets accurate results more often than can comfortably be ascribed to chance. It is difficult to believe that the credit for this should go to the tea-leaves or playing-cards, and a possible explanation of such success as is exhibited is that the tea-leaves or playing-cards, like the object used in psychometry, act as a catalyst to bring into play the *psi* faculty of someone who in fact has the gift of ESP. That certainly is the belief of one intelligent sensitive who possesses the *psi* faculty and manifests it in other ways. She places no store on what she sees in the hand of another; but she does believe that by holding it in her own hand and gazing at it, there is somehow triggered off in her her *psi* faculty which at times produces correct results. While with, say, tea-leaves no other explanation seems even remotely plausible, there is in palmistry a further factor which should not perhaps be ignored. Just as, to some extent, a person's character is reflected in his face and general mien, so it could be that it is reflected in his hands. We all know how quickly we get an impression of a person's character and mood from a glance at his face. If we are wise, we also know how unreliable such an impression may be; but we nevertheless continue to get such impressions. Most of us do not study other persons' hands so frequently or so closely as we study their faces. But the palmist does study palms closely; and it is not wholly absurd to suppose that possibly character and disposition are there reflected in much the same manner as they are in facial expressions, whether transitory or set. If this be so, it could explain some lucky shots at telling a person's character and history from the palms of his hands. It could not explain the foretelling of his future, save in so far as character and history are any guide to future probabilities.

Much the same considerations may apply to the so-called black box. It is a contraption looking rather like a small radio-set, with knobs and dials outside and inside a collection of wires which appear to lead nowhere and to do nothing. The manufacturers claim that it can be used diagnostically, and, if there be any justification in the claim, it defeats all rational understanding to discover what it can be. But a well-known man with some *psi* faculty says that, while he has no belief whatever in the black box, he does find that, by twiddling the knobs in the indicated manner, he is able to diagnose more effectively than if he does not do so, and he attributes this, probably correctly, to the catalytic effect on his *psi* faculty which these otherwise seemingly pointless operations seem to produce.

Crystal-gazing is another very ancient method of promoting ESP, and it probably does so in the catalytic manner, only, in this case, with the added factor of tiring the eyes, in much the same way as a hypnotist may tire the eyes of his patient as preliminary to administering suggestion. Crystal-gazing may, therefore, be a method of inducing a self-hypnosis, resulting in a very light trance, under which a latent *psi* faculty is brought into play. The method adopted by the seer is to gaze into a ball of clear glass. After a time, it is said that the glass appears to cloud over, after which the cloud disperses and the seer sees pictorially in the ball whatever it is for which he is searching, whether it be character-reading, or revelations of the past or foretellings of the future or the location of something which is lost. It is not always a glass ball that is used. Sometimes it is a bowl or a pool of water. In Egypt the seer gets a young boy and pours into the palm of his hand an ink-like liquid into which sometimes the seer, but more usually the boy, gazes until the cloud forms and then disperses revealing the significant picture.[2]

Dowsing and pendulum-swinging are both well-known ways of employing the *psi* faculty, or, perhaps one should say, of exciting or indicating that faculty. They have been used with considerable success, even in the commercial field, for discovering the whereabouts of water, minerals, oil and other things.

Traditionally the dowser looks for water and, for this purpose, equips himself with a Y-shaped hazel-twig. Grasping the arms of the Y in each hand in a certain way, he perambulates about the field in which it is hoped to find an underground supply of water. If he strikes water (invisible, because underground), the twig appears to twist in his hands. In fact it is his hands which move and the twig does no more than mark the movement of the hands. By this means the dowser claims to discover whether there is water there at all, and, if so, the direction and volume of its flow, the depth at which it lies and the quantity.

It is not thought that there is any virtue in the hazel-twig, save as a convenient indicator. The virtue lies in the dowser, and indicators other than hazel-twigs are used by some dowsers, the indicators being of various materials. Nor is it only water for which the dowser prospects. Oil and various minerals are among the quarries of some of them.

Another method to obtain the same results is the use of the pendulum. This usually consists of a weight at the end of a string or thread, about eighteen inches long. The diviner holds an end of the thread in his hand, letting the other end with the weight attached swing free. The pendulum thus formed swings in different patterns and with varying velocity, from side to side, clockwise, anti-clockwise, in wide or narrow ambits, fast or slowly. According to the way in which it swings the diviner claims to acquire the information for which he is seeking. One of the claims made for the pendulum is that by its use the sex of an embryo can be discovered.

The results are erratic; but sufficient success has been obtained to induce commercial enterprises to employ dowsers as well as metallurgists, geologists, engineers and other practitioners of the more orthodox sciences.

Divining, whether by dowsing or pendulum-swinging, is a mystery. Some who accept the phenomenon (and one is often driven to accept it) have sought an explanation in some as yet undiscovered physical property in the water or other object sought, operating in some normal but undiscovered, physical manner upon the operator, rather than in any *psi* faculty in the operator. The same might be said about many other variants of the *psi* faculty, which, if we ever do come to understand it, may turn out to be an as yet undiscovered extension of the known laws of physics. This is simply a complicated way of defining *psi* as something as yet unexplained. But to equate it in any way with the laws of physics becomes even more difficult in the face of a claim made by some diviners that they can successfully operate without ever leaving their own homes. The claim is that they can operate with a pendulum by swinging it over a map. By this means, so some of them claim, they can sit at a table in England with a map of South America in front of them and, given a map of sufficiently large scale, they can pinpoint on the map the course of, say, a vein of silver in Brazil. By the same method they claim to be able to trace the whereabouts of a missing person or of a body, usually combining the operation of pendulum-swinging with one of psychometry by holding in the other hand an article associated with the missing person. If such claims can be substantiated (and, though they require strict proof, we now know enough about *psi* to be cautious about denying the possibility of almost any claim), it is a clear indication that *psi* is as good an expression as any by which to denote the faculty, for it is as far removed as anything could be from anything attributable to the laws of physics as we now know them.

One of the manifestations of ESP which deserves mention on its own is the ability to 'read' the contents of a document or to tell the colour of an object, when the document or object is hidden from view. It is not an easy claim to test, for the arts of the conjurer have devised skilful means of counterfeiting the performance. Elaborate precautions have been taken to exclude any possibility of trickery. A message will be written by one person who does not divulge its content to anyone, but who seals it in several thicknesses of opaque envelopes and gives the package to another person who takes it to the experimenter who in turn gives it to the sensitive after the sensitive's eyes have been elaborately bandaged. The sensitive is kept under close observation, but, if the experiment is successful, nevertheless correctly gives the message concealed within the packet. Alternatively, a sensitive may be allowed to feel with the finger-tips a number of differently coloured sheets of paper, placed in such a position that he cannot see them. He is then asked to name the colours. In order to exclude any tactile impressions which he might otherwise receive, the sheets of paper are placed under another sheet of some transparent substance.

The French researcher, Richet, conducted a series of experiments some sixty years ago with a blindfolded sensitive. On one occasion she described the package as containing a picture of a soldier in uniform. When the package was opened, it was found not to contain any such picture, but instead to contain a sketch of a picture-frame. Subsequent inquiry of the person who had made up the package revealed that he had sketched the picture-frame surrounding the portrait of a soldier in uniform. What the sensitive had done was to describe the portrait which the person making up this package had *not* sketched, but at which he was looking while sketching the frame surrounding the portrait.[3]

Such incidents as these are extremely puzzling and show the elusive nature of the subject into which we are seeking to research. In this case the sensitive was clearly not 'seeing' the contents of the package. She was not exhibiting clairvoyance in the sense in which that word is usually used. Perhaps the incident should be categorised as a case of postcognition, in that what she 'saw' was something which had once been in the mind of the person who had made up the package. However it should be categorised, it is an example of abnormal awareness, not brought about by any normal means. It also has the advantage of excluding consideration of any sort of trickery such as a conjurer might employ to get a sight of the contents of the package. Short of collusion between the sensitive and the person who made up the package or of downright falsehood on the part of Richet, some exercise of the *psi* faculty provides the only explanation.

Another alleged psychic phenomenon is the aura. This, like the traditional halo, is an area of light more often said to be seen round the head, but also at times said to be round the whole body. It seems impossible to prove whether such experiences are subjective or objective, but so many persons claim to see auras that it would be rash to deny the reality of the experience. One must also take into account the fact that something must have given rise to the tradition of denoting a saint in a picture by giving him a halo. Most sensitives who have given evidence of possession of the *psi* faculty in other ways claim to see auras. But many a person who gives no other indication of possessing ESP also claims to see auras. If the aura in fact exists, it seems to be possessed by most persons, if not by every person, and not to be the exclusive prerogative of the saintly. But the colour of the aura seems to vary, and there is no marked consistency in the descriptions of auras given by different persons. The colour seems to vary not only in the eyes of the beholder, but also from person to person round whom it is viewed. It seems to vary, moreover, according to the health and mood of the person viewed, and those who claim to see auras seem to place the same sort of reliance on the colour and extent of the aura as indicating health and mood as we all tend to place on facial expression and general demeanour.

The latest[4] alleged manifestations of the *psi* faculty are those made fashionable by Mr Uri Geller, taking the form of twisting forks and other metal objects and causing watches to stop or to go, all by the power of thought alone. Since Mr Uri Geller was televised, a large number of claims to have performed similar feats have been made from many quarters. They will none of them be examined here, since they are the subject of other investigations and judgement had better be deferred.[5] But, although the exploits recently claimed are startling, they do not appear to be essentially different in kind from experiments in telekinesis (TK)[6] whereby it is claimed that one can move objects at a distance by thought alone and without any physical contact. Dr Rhine's experiments under strict test conditions at Duke University have met with a fair measure of success. It is claimed that some persons can influence the fall of dice by TK, or swing a balanced needle (such as a compass-needle); and experiments are now going on to influence the groupings of bacteria.

Nothing will here be said about UFOs (unidentified

flying objects), for whether or not such can be substantiated, there is nothing to indicate that they belong to the realm of psychical research beyond the fact that they are unexplained. The object of this chapter is to give some idea of the variety and range of the manifestations of the *psi* faculty, at least in so far as the claims made deserve to be considered seriously.

9

HEALING

MANY of the phenomena which interest psychical researchers seem, apart from their intrinsic interest as unexplained events, to be trivial and purposeless. It is, therefore, a relief to turn to healing which being also largely unexplained has no less intrinsic interest and is also utilitarian and beneficial. Healing bestrides the frontiers both between mind and body and also between the natural sciences, psychical research and theology. The reader, therefore, is warned that from this point onwards he will not be able to escape altogether from theological considerations. They will be presented with as much objectivity as can be mustered and are largely common to Christianity as a whole; but, since the author is an Anglican, they may sometimes have an Anglican slant. The reader is forewarned and can, therefore, if need be, muster his own critical defensive faculties accordingly.

For our purposes types of healing may be conveniently considered under five main headings, namely: healing by *materia medica*; healing by direct divine intervention; the Church's ministry of healing; the charismatic gift of healing; and the type of healing which spiritualists believe is ministered from beyond the grave. This categorisation is one simply of convenience and it will be found that the categories overlap. It should, however, be made clear at the outset that, in the Christian view, all healing of whatever category, is of God.

Of all types of healing, that with which we are most familiar is healing by means of *materia medica*. In it are included the art, skill and knowledge of the physician, of the surgeon, of the psychiatrist, and of the ancillary medical services, such as dentistry, nursing, physiotherapy, and much else. The Christian, nevertheless, maintains that it is all of God, and that the practitioners in all branches of *materia medica*, when they achieve success, do so only as God's human agents, whether or not they recognise the fact. No. surgeon, for example, ever mends a broken limb. All that he does is to place the two ends of the broken bone in the right juxtaposition for them to grow together and rejoin. The process of growth, like the creation of life in the first instance, is within the control of Man only to the extent that he can encourage or discourage it. He cannot himself effect it. The property of growth, like life itself, is bestowed by God, and it is bestowed by him on some things and not on others. It is bestowed on human tissue, for example; it is not bestowed on rock, so that it is useless to place the two ends of a broken piece of rock together in the hope that they will join and become one. If man places the ends of living bone together, God joins them because he has given them life; but, if man places two pieces of rock together, nothing happens, for God has not given them that property. Man's part in the healing process is comparatively trifling. It is confined to co-operating with God who alone does the real work of healing.

God is a Trinity. Man, being made in the image of God,[1] is a trinity also, consisting of body, mind and soul. What precisely mind is has yet to be discovered. It seems to be centred in the brain; but it is not itself the brain.

As was suggested in Chapter 6, it is perhaps best conceived as an activity—as a two-way activity, being the
action of the body on the soul and the action of the
soul on the body. The relationship between these three
constituent parts of Man is so intimate that whatever
affects any one part directly also indirectly affects the
other two parts. Those who practise medicine recognise
that body and mind affect each other and have em-
braced within the ambit of medicine the healing of the
mind so that psychiatry finds its place within the art
and science of medicine. The existence and importance
of the soul are not so generally recognised as truly a part
of medicine and the ordinary medical practitioner claims
no expertise in this field. But recognition is by no means
wholly denied, and so we have hospital chaplains as
well as physicians and surgeons, and by many the rôle
of the chaplain in the total process of healing is
recognised.

It seems to be part of the divine plan that the creatures of earth should in large measure manage their own
affairs and the affairs of earth, with Man in general
control.[2] Inasmuch as Man is both material and spiritual
he may have to employ both material and spiritual
means to achieve his ends. It is, therefore, natural and
right that *materia medica* should play a very large part
in the process of healing and, inasmuch as we are all
members one of another,[3] it is also right that we should
rely on each other for the appropriate application of
materia medica. But, inasmuch as our knowledge, though
growing daily, is limited, there are limits, albeit shrink-
ing daily, to what can be achieved by *materia medica*
alone. It is at this point that God steps in and supplies
some other method of healing. He has been called 'the
God of gaps', a derisory term intended to signify that

those who are so foolish as to believe in his existence with equal folly attribute to him anything which passes their own understanding, and that, as human understanding increases, so the gaps to be filled by this supposed God decrease. Perhaps the scoffers are more right than they suppose. It may be that that is exactly how God acts. Like any good parent dealing with a child, God leaves us to do for ourselves whatever is within our competence; but, for those things which are beyond our present competence, God is ready to step in. When he does so, and when we recognise that he has done so, we call it a miracle, if we are theistically minded. If we are atheistically minded, we call it (in the context of medicine) a spontaneous remission. It is not a very helpful term and indicates no more than that the cause of the healing is inexplicable except by the one explanation which the atheist must reject, namely, by attributing it to God. The theist, however, can also easily slip into error by marvelling over-much at a miracle, while forgetting that all healing is from God and is equally an object for wonder, and is, in effect, only an extension of the greatest miracle of all, which occurred at the Creation, when God made everything out of nothing.

By *miracle*, then, we mean the intervention by God, filling up the gaps, in some manner other than by the means of human agency. It may be that in Biblical times there were more miracles than there are today, for the gaps in human knowledge and skills were then much wider and, therefore, the need for God's direct intervention was greater. But there is no reason to suppose that miracles ceased with the Acts of the Apostles. Those who are tempted so to think should read the life of Dorothy Kerin,[4] which brings us right down to modern times. Hers is a very well-attested case, or, rather, series of cases. She was both the recipient of miraculous healing and also the agent through whom it was bestowed on others. If she had been a Roman Catholic, she would almost certainly have been canonised, but the Church of England has never instituted the machinery for the official recognition of a saint, and she was in fact an Anglican.

She was born in 1889. At the age of fifteen she contracted diphtheria, and thereafter was forced to spend much of her time in bed. Her health rapidly declined and in December, 1911, tubercular peritonitis was diagnosed and her condition pronounced hopeless. In February, 1912, when she was twenty-two, she became blind and deaf and then apparently unconscious and on the 18th February, 1912, her end seemed very near. Those who were at her bedside thought that she had died and for eight minutes discerned no sign of breathing. Perhaps she did die; but suddenly she sat up in bed and exclaimed, 'I must follow that light', the while she looked at something which no one else could see. She got out of bed and walked unaided out of the room and then returned, and, despite the protestations of those around, she insisted on eating a hearty meal of cold meat from the larder. All sign of wastage had disappeared and she seemed in all respects to be a healthy young woman. After a thorough medical examination she was declared to be entirely free from tuberculosis. Thereafter she devoted her whole life to the healing of others, and many a cure is attributed to her agency. Finally she founded her home of healing, a nursing-home at Burrswood, near East Grinstead. In addition to a fully qualified medical and nursing staff, there is a chapel and a chaplain, and the Church's ministry of healing is administered both to the resident patients and to visitors to the chapel where a service of healing takes place three times a week. Dorothy Kerin eventually died in 1964 at the age of seventy-four; but her work continues at Burrswood and her inspiration over a very wide field.

What happened to Dorothy Kerin herself comes in the category of direct divine intervention, as would also the miracle-cures which draw pilgrims in their thousands to places such as Lourdes. As at Lourdes, so with Dorothy Kerin: no human agency was involved in the act of healing which brought about the immediate and complete spontaneous remission in so dramatic a form. But the work which she founded and which is carried on at Burrswood is an example of our third category of healing, namely, the Church's ministry of healing. It is a ministry which flourished during the first three centuries of the Christian Church, but which declined thereafter. It may or may not be coincidence that its decline coincides with the formal recognition and legal establishment of the Church under Constantine. There is no reason why establishment itself should have this effect; but, whereas before establishment it required considerable dedication to be a Christian, official recognition of the Church brought about a large influx of undedicated persons who were happy to climb onto the ecclesiastical band-wagon. The fervour of the dedicated few was diluted by large numbers of undedicated conformists, and healing, which had until then played a prominent part in the spreading of the Gospel, went into a decline. Whether or not this was a case of *post hoc, propter hoc*, the decline occurred; but the last few years have seen a considerable revival in England of the Church's ministry of healing.[5]

This ministry is based directly on our Lord's command, 'Go ye into all the world and preach the gospel to every living creature . . . These signs shall follow them that believe: In my name shall they cast out devils; they shall speak with tongues, . . . they shall lay hands on the sick, and they shall recover.'[6] It was a repeated command and recorded in several places in the Gospels. It is odd that obedience to it should have lapsed for so long, especially having regard to the fact that the command to take bread and wine was given only once, at the Institution of the Last Supper, and yet that has become the central act of worship for the great bulk of Christendom. One of the reasons for the lapse in the practice may be a certain diffidence in presuming to emulate Christ. But, if so, it ignores his own statement, 'Verily, verily, I say unto you, he that believeth on me, the works that I do shall he do also; and greater works than these shall he do.'[7]

The method usually adopted for administering this type of healing is the strictly Biblical one of the laying on of hands[8] with prayer and sometimes anointing with oil.[9] The service is for preference conducted in church; but, if necessary, at the place where the patient is. Sometimes someone else will come for the laying-on of hands as proxy for the patient.

The theological *rationale* for this ministry may be stated quite shortly. God's Creation was a perfect creation; 'God saw everything that he had made, and behold, it was very good.'[10] Man, being part of that Creation, was perfect also. But, by disobedience, man fell, and thus imperfection entered into what before was perfect. It is, however, God's will that all should be perfect again and that man should be whole and holy (the two words are etymologically connected). In the person of Jesus, God was incarnate in order to make perfection possible, and Jesus, as perfect man, made man whole again when opportunity arose. When he ascended once more to the Father, he left behind his Body, the Church, to continue here the works which he began on earth; and that is why he repeatedly commanded his disciples to heal and sought to assure them that they had the power to do so. How it happens is not vouchsafed. But God, who is concerned with wholeness, is concerned with the whole man, body, mind and soul, and he operates on the whole man, that is, on every part of him, body, mind and soul. Why, then, it may be asked, does not healing always take place? Again, we do not know. But we do know that God is perfect and is, therefore, a perfectionist, who will not do what is less than perfect. He will bestow on the recipient whatever is the greatest blessing which the recipient is capable of receiving with advantage. This may be, and sometimes is, bodily wholeness; but not always. The Church, therefore, in its ministry of healing, while praying that the patient may be made whole in body, mind and soul, prays that God will make him whole, *as he would have him be*, and prays thus in the confidence that some blessing will be bestowed, that it may be the blessing of healing, but that, if it is not that, it will, nevertheless, be the greatest blessing appropriate to that recipient. It must be emphasised that whoever is ministering at a service of healing is doing so on behalf of the Body of Christ, that is, of the whole Church, and makes no claim himself to be endowed with any special healing virtue. This type of healing is thus to be distinguished from healing by someone with the charismatic gift.

The charismatic gift of healing is (or should be) recognised by the Church as fully as the Church's own ministry, for it is one of the gifts of the Spirit enumerated by St Paul,[11] and it is a special gift, among the diversity of gifts, and not all persons have received the same gift. It is sometimes known as the healing touch, and Dorothy Kerin, among many others, had it. Those who possess it have no idea how it works, and the testimony that it does work comes in the main from patients who are certain that they have benefited from it.

The fourth type of healing is that which the spiritualists claim is administered by the spirits of the departed through the mediumship of someone on earth. It is the claim which is made by Mr Harry Edwards among others, and he is convinced that the healing comes through him from deceased doctors.

No one need doubt the sincerity with which the practitioners (if that be the right word) in this type of healing hold these views, nor the devotion with which they have dedicated their lives to relieving sickness, nor the self-effacement with which they claim to be no more than channels to enable others (the departed) to work through them; nor need we deny to them their measure of undoubted success. It is, however, permissible to question whether they have rightly interpreted what is happening. One alternative possible explanation is that, without knowing it, they have the charismatic gift. Another more prosaic explanation is that success, when it occurs, is due to the suggestibility of the patient. Their own explanation, that they are mediums through whom deceased doctors work, is one which is not readily accepted by many churchfolk, for churchfolk tend to regard everything connected with spiritualism with deep suspicion and even as satanic, and need sometimes to be reminded that our Lord himself said, 'He that is not against us is for us.'[12] The views of these practitioners are not to be dismissed so lightly. As to the charge of

satanism; this was brought by the Pharisees against
Christ himself and was sternly repudiated in the words,
'If Satan cast out Satan, he is divided against himself:
how then can his kingdom stand?'[13] And, as to the claims
that deceased doctors are responsible for this work of
healing; there is nothing fundamentally contrary to
Christian doctrine in this. In the Collect for Michaelmas
Day[14] we pray, 'Mercifully grant that as thy holy Angels
always do thee service in heaven, so by thy appointment
they may succour and defend us on earth.' Deceased
doctors are not angels; but, like angels, they are now in
a world of spirit, and, if one type of spirit can intervene
in the affairs of earth, there is no reason to suppose that
another type cannot do so also.

In any attempt to assess healing or to attribute it to
any particular cause, great caution is needed. It is difficult enough in the context of orthodox medicine. It is even
more difficult when the mode of healing is unorthodox.
The very fact of healing is by no means always easy to
establish; its cause is even less easy. There can be little
doubt that, whatever the method, orthodox or unorthodox, suggestion can play an enormous part in bringing
about the cure. The strength of suggestion is evidenced
by hypnotism. Its value is recognised by the orthodox
medical practitioner who prescribes a mere *placebo*,
often with great effect. It may well be that many
a medicament in which the practitioner himself has faith
in fact has been a mere *placebo* and, but for the suggestibility of the patient, inspired by the confidence of the
doctor, would have contributed nothing to the patient's
recovery. *Recovery* is itself an ill-defined term. It may
amount to the complete eradication of the cause of the
patient's disease; but it may be no more than an allevia-
tion of the symptoms, good so far as it relieves the patient

of the painful effects of the disease, but dangerous in that it masks the disease so that the symptoms no longer fulfil their necessary function as a warning. These considerations apply to orthodox medicine. They apply with at least equal force to less orthodox methods of healing. But there is enough evidence[15] to indicate that it is not only orthodox medicine that is followed by recovery. The laying-on of hands, whether by the Church, or by those with the charismatic gift or by spiritualists, is followed sufficiently often by improvement in the patient to render it reasonable to suppose that in some way the cure has been effected in the manner claimed; and to term such recovery as *spontaneous remission* is to say no more than that the recovery is unexpected and to the speaker inexplicable.

Nor does it help to describe these non-medical methods as *faith-healing*. It begs the issue and implicitly assumes that suggestion alone is responsible. In fact the part that faith plays, though probably great in both orthodox and unorthodox medicine, is largely an unknown factor, even theologically. The importance of faith is emphasised again and again in the Gospels, and yet it is clear that it is not invariably a *sine qua non*. No one expected either Lazarus[16] or the son of the widow of Nain[17] to be raised from the dead; faith seems to have played no part in the performance of those miracles. But elsewhere we are told that Christ did not many mighty works there because of their unbelief.[18]

It is, too, difficult to know how far healing of any sort is attributable to purely physical causes, to psychological causes, to psychic causes or to spiritual causes. The physical, the psychological, the psychic and the spiritual overlap and interlock at so many points that one cannot disentangle the threads and it is reasonable to suspect that no hard and fast boundaries exist between them. The one point on which most persons, even those with the most divergent views, will agree is that healing is seldom successful unless it aims at the health of the whole man. This certainly includes the body and the mind, and those who claim that it also includes the soul can produce much to support the claim.[19]

POSSESSION AND EXORCISM

THE practice of exorcism presupposes the existence not merely of a spiritual entity, but of one in the wrong place whose removal can be effected by spiritual means. Exorcism, therefore, is a religious exercise which may in fact be dealing with something psychic, but which is designed to deal with something spiritual which is thought to be acting contrary to God's will and to the discomfort of some part of God's material Creation. The spiritual entity with which exorcism seeks to deal may be actually satanic, and some persons claim that this is always the case. But, whether or not this is an exaggeration, the entity is always in some degree evil in that it is in the nature of a trespasser, being somewhere where it ought not to be, seeking to take actual possession, or at least to make use, of a person, an animal, a place or an object which does not belong to it.

Although many churchfolk join forces with many others, including natural scientists, in denying the existence of the psychic, belief in possession and in the efficacy of exorcism has never ceased to be an orthodox part of the Church's teaching. There is ample support for it in the New Testament. To mention but a few instances: there is the episode of the exorcism of the demoniac (or demoniacs) near the Sea of Galilee with the puzzling account of our Lord's suffering the legion

of devils to go into the herd of swine;[1] there is the exorcism
of the boy immediately after our Lord's Transfiguration;[2]
there is the exorcism of the dumb man possessed by a
devil;[3] and there is the account of Paul's exorcising the
damsel possessed of a spirit of divination.[4] For centuries
the Church regarded exorcism, like healing (with which
it is closely associated), as a part of its task as the Body of
Christ to continue the work which he performed when
on earth. The office of exorcist was recognised as one
of the minor Orders in the Church, and is still so recognised in the Church of Rome, but not in the Church of
England or in the Orthodox Church. But exorcism was
never confined to persons holding the office of exorcist.
Indeed, it has usually been regarded as an especially
appropriate function for any bishop or priest, while not
confined to them. In the East it is looked on as a charismatic gift, often bestowed on the laity, and in the West
the power to exorcise has never been regarded as
bestowed exclusively on ordained persons. In the Middle
Ages some restraint on exorcism by all and sundry was
thought advisable and, by canon law, the right to exorcise
was restricted to persons licensed by the bishop to do so.
This restriction was repeated in England after the
Reformation by canon 72 of the Anglican canons of 1603.
With the dawning of the so-called age of reason the
practice of exorcism became so rare that canon 72 ceased
to be of the same practical importance, and in the recent
revision of canon law in the Church of England the
canons of 1603 (with one irrelevant exception) were
wholly repealed, including canon 72, and nothing was
said about exorcism in the revised canons which have
taken their place. The enacted canons are, however, only
a part of canon law, and a large part of canon law
remains unwritten, and it is thought that, by virtue of

pre-Reformation canon law (of which much is still in force in England), the permission of the bishop should first be obtained before the exorcism of a person is effected, but that no such permission is needed before the exorcism of a place.[5]

The past decade,[6] however, has seen a considerable revival of both the ministry of healing and of exorcism. The renewal of exorcism is due in part to a growing recognition of the immanence of the non-material within the material world and the view that the age of reason followed by the age of science had gone too far in categorising the many old beliefs and practices as mere superstition. There is, in fact, a growing recognition of the validity of the warning given by the writer of the Epistles to the Ephesians[7] that 'we wrestle not against flesh and blood, but against principalities, against powers, against the rulers of the darkness of this world, against spiritual wickedness in high places', in other words, that our true adversaries are spiritual ones. It is also due in part to a welcome revulsion against excessive materialism, a revulsion which elsewhere has unfortunately manifested itself unpleasantly in a revival of the practices of black magic and witchcraft which in turn have, it is thought, led to an increase in satanic activity, including possession.

It is not to be thought that witchcraft is to be equated with possession or is necessarily satanic. There are, in fact, two sorts of witchcraft, black and white. Black magic and black witchcraft are both not merely evil, but profess to be evil and set out to be evil. Those who indulge in them are, therefore, deliberately encouraging the satanic and deliberately laying themselves wide open to evil influences. They may, therefore, be a ready prey for evil forces seeking to possess them. White witchcraft, on the other hand, is comparatively harmless. It is really a religion whose adherents do not seek to harm anyone or anything. It is a hotch-potch of remnants of old nature-religions mixed up with Zoroastrianism. Like all magic, it is an attempt to gain control over natural forces, but, in the case of white magic, by harmless methods and without evil intent. Neither witchcraft nor magic can receive further examination here, and it is not politic to give too much publicity to some of their practices; but they should not be dismissed as complete nonsense, for, despite some of the trappings in which they are wrapped, the psychical researcher will often recognise in their practices a recurrence of psychic activities with which he is already familiar in other contexts.

The term *possession* is an imprecise one. Its manifestations can range from what appears to be the complete taking over and occupation of a person's body and mind by an alien entity to the simple inspiring of a person for good or for ill. It can be a prolonged occupation, or it can be temporary or spasmodic, when it is sometimes called *obsession* rather than *possession*. It is to be found in circumstances far removed from those which call for the intervention of an exorcist. Pentecostalism provides an example of what looks like possession. It may well be possession by the Holy Spirit. It is in any event benevolent, and, far from being in the nature of a trespass, it is invited by the subject. It may manifest itself in glossalalia, that is, in the 'speaking with tongues', usually in speech which is completely unknown and unrecognisable, but which sounds as though it has a consistency and formation of its own, but which, uninterpreted, has no meaning for the listeners. The gift of interpreting these utterances is, however, claimed by the adherents of Pentecostalism to be one of the gifts of the spirit. But occasionally the utterances are in a recognisable language, though one unknown to the speaker. The speaker appears to be in ecstasy and sometimes indulges in 'holy shakes', rolling about on the floor and shaking violently. It is not easy to differentiate between this type of religious ecstasy and hysteria. But it is at worst harmless, being directed God-ward. At best it is inspired by God. Those who have not experienced it should be as cautious about dismissing it summarily as they should be about dismissing any mystical experience. To the Pentecostalist, as to the mystic, his experience is very real and very valuable, and it may be that those of us who have not shared the experience are as incapable of evaluating it as someone born blind is incapable of evaluating colour.

Another very different type of possession is that which seems to occur with some mediums when they go into trance and appear to be taken over either by the entity with whom they are seeking contact or by the medium's guide.[8] This, too, is not a case of trespass, the communicating entities come by invitation. There is, however, the danger of an uninvited entity's slipping in unobserved, and there is also the danger of some invited guest's overstaying his welcome. The case might then become one for the exorcist. But the occasions on which this happens seem to be very rare.

All cases of apparent possession present the observer with the problem of determining whether he is faced with a case of true possession or with something else. He must be alive to the possibility that it is some form of hysteria or delusional insanity. He must also be alive to the possibility of its being a secondary personality. Equally, the psychologist should be alive to the possibility that what he believes to be a case of hysteria, delusional insanity or secondary personality may in fact be a case of possession. Indeed, it is pertinent to ask whether there *is* such a phenomenon as the secondary personality. It is as pertinent to ask that question as it is to ask whether there is such a phenomenon as possession. The Jekyll-and-Hyde phenomenon is by no means unknown[9] and the outward manifestation would lead one to suppose that at different times utterly different personalities are inhabiting the same body, turn and turn about. The psychologist who does not believe in possession may term the phenomenon one of secondary personality; but there is little to indicate whether it is truly that or a case of possession and the term employed will depend very much on the presuppositions of the person using it. If anything, the indications are that possession is the more probable explanation. One such indication is that exorcism can be effective, and, even allowing for the power on the patient of suggestion, it is sometimes more easy to believe that a trespassing entity can be expelled by exorcism than that a secondary personality can be suppressed by the ceremony. Another indication that possession is the true explanation is that sometimes the patient gives utterance in a language unknown to him. This points to his being possessed by another entity, and the same is true when a medium in trance speaks in a language unknown to her or an automatist writes in one. In all these cases the use of a language unknown to the speaker or writer is an indication that some third party is communicating. One is tempted to regard it as a conclusive indication; but the more one sees of the psychic the more cautious one becomes about regarding anything as conclusive. There is always the possibility that some form of ESP is at work. It is a possibility rather than a probability, and the use of a foreign language unknown to the speaker can reasonably be regarded as a strong indication of possession as against the theory of a secondary personality.

The cases recorded in the Bible and catergorised there as cases of possession have been rationalised as cases of insanity, epilespsy or some other physical or psychological illness, and such rationalisation was common in the wave of materialism which marked the aftermath of Darwin's influence. It is still common among those who in religion call themselves modernists. But, with the growing awareness of the reality of spiritual and psychic dimensions, such an attitude is today less common. It is obvious that Jesus himself believed in the demonic and in possession,[10] and however legitimate it may be to attribute to his contemporaries an ignorance of modern medicine which could lead them to mistake illness for possession, it is not so easy to attribute the same ignorance or confusion to one so manifestly aware of the spiritual and the psychic as was our Lord.

In cases of apparent demonic possession of a person, that person's whole personality can appear to change radically and to change very much for the worse. The current[11] film, *The Exorcist*, is based on a novel of the same name by William Peter Blatty which was itself based on a notorious case of apparent demonic possession in Maryland, U.S.A., in 1949.[12] It is an example of an extreme case of violent, prolonged and complete possession, accompanied by other psychic phenomena, such as raps, levitation and movements of furniture. But, although such extreme cases are rare, they are not unknown.

The actual ceremony of exorcism varies from time to time and place to place, according to circumstances, including the proficiency and the religious views of the exorcist; but essentially all exorcisms are the same. The exorcist's first task should, if possible, be diagnosis in order to discover, if he can, whether he is faced with a genuine case of possession and whether it is demonic. In short, he should discover as much about the case as possible. This will include obtaining the case-history of the patient. Some exorcists believe themselves to be gifted with ESP, enabling them to have a direct apprehension of what it is which is facing them. Others have been known to employ the services of someone else with ESP, perhaps with mediumistic gifts, to supply the information. Others, who perhaps regard everything psychic with horror and as diabolic, will have no truck with such an approach. Once satisfied that the case is one of possession (itself not an easy task), they assume that it must be demonic and act accordingly. The next step, not always practicable, is to obtain a request from the patient for exorcism. In a case of complete possession this will not be forthcoming, because the possessing entity has taken over and wishes to remain in control. But in less extreme cases (cases of obsession rather than of possession), where, for instance, the patient is aware merely of being worried and oppressed by some outside agency, the initial approach for relief may well come from the patient himself. Having decided that exorcism is appropriate, the exorcist prepares himself for it, certainly by prayer, and probably by fasting, confession and Holy Communion. He also prepares in the same manner those who are to assist him.

When all is ready, the actual exorcism begins. It takes place, if possible, in a church in the presence only of the patient, the exorcist and his assistants. These should include persons who are prepared and able, if need be, to restrain the patient physically, should he become violent, as sometimes happens. For the same reason the patient should be seated comfortably in such a manner that, should he throw himself about, he is less likely to harm himself.

If, as is more often the case, the exorcist is a priest, he is likely to have another priest as one of his assistants and they will be clad in cassock, cotta or surplice and violet stole. They will have a crucifix and holy water.

After reciting the Lord's Prayer and other prayers and reading from the Bible, the exorcist comes to what is intended to be the effective part of the ceremony. It consists in a command, firmly given, in the Name of the Father and of the Son and of the Holy Spirit, and it is addressed directly to the invading entity or entities and bids them depart from the patient and, harming no one, to return to the place appointed for them. Sometimes the exorcist lays his hands on the patient's head and sometimes he sprinkles him with holy water and sometimes he breathes out deeply. Sometimes he demands of the invading entity his name.

After (as it is hoped) the exorcism proper has been completed successfully, more prayers are said. Bearing in mind the parable of the unclean spirit who returned and found the place empty, swept and garnished and entered in again with seven other spirits more wicked than himself,[18] one of the prayers should be that the patient may be filled with the Holy Spirit. Another may well be for the guardianship of the patient by the holy angels. Finally, a blessing is given.

In the form of exorcism given in *The Findings of a Commission convened by the Bishop of Exeter*,[14] the exorcism proper includes the command (in the Name of the Trinity) to 'every evil spirit' that 'harming no one, you depart from this creature of God—and return to the place appointed you, there to remain for ever'. This, it is arguable, is both theologically and practically doubt-ful in exactly this form. The command to depart and to do no harm is unexceptionable. So also is the command to go to the place appointed, always assuming that there *is* such a place. It would be interesting to know on what authority this assumption rests. But the command 'there to remain for ever' presupposes that the invading entity is diabolic and wholly beyond hope of redemption. That is a serious presupposition and one wonders whether it ought to be made. If one is to assume that each entity has an appointed place (which is doubtful), it would seem more charitable as well as more cautious to com-mand return to it 'until the appointed time'.

All who do not dismiss the whole concept of possession as false will agree that a vitally important part of exorcism consists in the after-care of the patient. It is not enough to rest content with the expulsion of an invader. It is necessary also to build up the patient to resist further inva-sions, and, in particular, to see that the vacuum formed by the departure of the invader is quickly filled, and kept filled, by what is good so that there is no room for a further invasion. The original invasion may be regarded as either psychic or spiritual. The expulsion of the invader is spiritual, being performed solely by God, the exorcist being no more than the channel through which God works. The rehabilitation of the patient also is spiritual, for it consists in his being so filled with spiritual virtue that evil can find no place in him.

The exorcism of a place, such as a haunted house, is essentially the same as the exorcism of a person and follows much the same form with appropriate variations. There is, however, this difference, that whereas the adverse possession of a person is likely to be possession by an evil entity, inasmuch as trespassing is evil, the haunting of a place may well be by a misguided, rather than an evil, entity. It is for this reason that sometimes the services of a medium are enlisted, and sometimes the medium's verdict is that the haunting is by a deceased person who does not realise that he is dead. The medium then tries to explain to him that he *is* dead and, if the attempt is successful, the deceased is persuaded to accept his new-found status and to depart to a more appropriate sphere, whereupon the haunting ceases. If this be not pure fantasy, it provides a good example of an instance when exorcism would be inappropriate, and an exorcism which presupposes that the entity is evil and should be banished for ever 'to the place appointed', would be grossly inappropriate and most uncharitable.

Just as the exorcism of a person is probably followed by prayers and a blessing, so is the exorcism of a place. In neither case, however, can one be certain that a further exorcism will not be required. This is especially true of the exorcism of a place. It is not necessarily a reflection on the efficacy of exorcism. There may be more than one invading entity about, for one type of psychic infestation seems to attract others. The exorcism may have been partially successful in that one entity has been expelled; but others may remain, or the first one may return.

The subject cannot be left without a warning. Exorcism may be dangerous. It may be dangerous to the exorcist and those assisting him, and, in the case of the exorcism of a person, it may be dangerous to the patient. The danger to the patient was recognised even in medieval times and was the reason for the canonical requirement to obtain the permission of the bishop before attempting the exorcism of a person as distinct from a place. A mentally unbalanced person who is not possessed may easily be still further deranged by the impressive (but, in his case, unnecessary) ceremony of exorcism.

It may be dangerous physically, spiritually and psychologically. Physically, there is always the possibility of violence on the part of the person possessed, or, rather through him on the part of the possessing entity. Spiritually it may be dangerous, because the possessing entity may seek to find a home within one of those concerned in carrying out the exorcism. Cases in which this appears to have happened have been known. As has been said, it may be dangerous psychologically to the patient. Great care is required where the case may be complex. Some patients give the appearance of being sufferers from, say, genuine schizophrenia, but also of being psychic. The psychiatrist who has diagnosed schizophrenia may be quite right so far as his diagnosis goes. But it may not go far enough. The patient may also be spasmodically possessed. Alternatively, he may appear at times to be possessed, and yet in fact not be possessed. Such cases present great problems and call for great care in treatment. An attempt at exorcism could well exacerbate the schizophrenia and undo such good as the psychiatrist has effected. Clearly, consultation is highly desirable between the psychiatrist and those contemplating exorcism. The latter are probably willing that such consultation should take place. The psychiatrist may not be so willing (though some are). What should happen is something about which it is impossible to generalise; but such a situation emphasises one of the difficulties and dangers involved.

During the past two centuries or so exorcism may have been unjustly neglected. Today the pendulum may be swinging too far in the other direction and the resort to exorcism may be too frequent and too readily adopted by those who are lacking in the necessary experience and judgement. Often confession (auricular or otherwise), absolution and the laying-on of hands for healing will suffice. Sometimes obsession of the patient by a deceased person may call, not for exorcism, but for the pastoral care (so far as it can be given) both of the living patient and of the obsessing deceased.[15] In short, exorcism of a person (as distinct from a place) should be regarded as a last resort, like surgery, and not to be lightly undertaken, while even exorcism of a place should have regard to the possibility that the haunting entity may be in need of help. One way of providing this help is by the saying of a requiem, for the repose of the troubled soul.

CHRISTIANITY AND PSYCHICAL RESEARCH

SO far in this book we have been concerned with a review of the field of psychical research. It is a wide field and not all of it has been covered. But enough has been covered to enable the reader who comes fresh to the subject to form some view of the nature of the psychic. It is an interesting field of exploration. But it is more than that; it is important in its bearing on both natural science and religion. In this chapter we shall consider primarily the relationship between psychical research and Christianity.

As has been said already, it is (in my view and in that of many others) idle to deny the existence of some psychic phenomena, notably telepathy, precognition, apparitions and poltergeists. Their explanation, however, is quite another matter. But whatever may be their explanation, all these phenomena have one thing in common; they reveal that the ordinary laws of physics as at present understood, useful though they are for the ordinary affairs of life on this planet, do not tell the whole story and present but a partial picture of existence. One can go further and state that, if but a single psychic pheno- menon can be proved to have occurred, that alone is enough to require a revision of our formulation of the laws of physics or else an acknowledgement that there is a dimension beyond the physical. This, in turn, has a bearing on religion, for our religion depends in large measure, if not totally, on our experience of the Universe around us, even while it is concerned with matters beyond this life and this Universe. The here-and-now is of necessity our starting-point, however widely we may range in the realms of deduction and speculation, and, if psychic phenomena occur, our here-and-now is different from the picture presented by an orthodox formulation of the laws of physics. To the materialistically minded natural scientist, therefore, we would say, 'Look at the evidence. If you find there nothing to suggest that the psychic exists, you are justified in ignoring it and resting content with what you already know and with the formulation of the laws which you have deduced there-from. If, however, you find enough to suggest that the psychic may be a fact, encourage its further exploration as you would encourage the further exploration of any other possibility. If, however, you go further and discover that the psychic is, as is claimed, a reality, then you must consider its bearing on the laws of physics which you have already learnt, for it is clear that, as at present expressed, they are inadequate to explain the nature of things.'

The theologian, too, has a duty to look at the evidence. Hitherto, all too often, he has either ignored the psychic altogether, or dismissed it as nonsense, or has acknow-ledged its reality, but shunned it as being of the devil. To ignore it is odd in those of whom the majority may be expected by profession to believe in a non-material dimen-sion to Creation. For a Christian theologian to treat it as nonsense is to demonstrate how deeply he has been infected by the comparatively modern and now slightly

outdated wave of secular materialism. To regard it as a
diabolical reality is at least logical and is to adopt an
attitude which deserves to be taken seriously. It is, however, an attitude which those adopting it may reasonably
be challenged to defend. There are arguments to support
their view, just as there are arguments against it. But
they both require to be stated and examined. If arguments can be advanced to show that in some respects
psychical research is inimical to religion, arguments can
also be advanced to show that it is of value to religion.
Let us see if we can strike some sort of balance-sheet.

On the credit side for psychical research several items
can be put; but there is one of quite outstanding value
to the cause of religion. If psychical phenomena be
established as realities, it is clearly shown that what we
now call the material does not comprise the whole of existence. There is a dimension beyond what at present we
call the purely material. It may be spiritual, or it may be
psychic; but it is, in terms of current physics, non-
material, and this is the essence of religion's claim. If the
material be all that exists, then Christianity, together with
most, if not all, other religions, is false. If there be something beyond the material, then present-day materialism
is false. That it is materialism which has been shown
to be false is the claim of many psychical researchers.
The claim must not be overstated. There may be a
spiritual dimension as well as a psychic dimension. We
may ultimately discover that there is no essential difference between the material, the psychic and the spiritual;
that they shade imperceptibly into each other; and that
it is simply a question of degree. But the terms, *material*,
psychical and *spiritual* are convenient terms for denoting
three broad categories, the psychical being the middle
category, shading off at one end into the material and

at the other end into the spiritual. With a recognition of the reality of the psychic factor and with the advent of more knowledge concerning it, we may eventually reframe the laws of physics so that they take account of the psychic as well as of the physical. If we do, it is quite likely that our extended understanding will be regarded as an extension of physics and it will be forgotten that it is the psychic which has given rise to the extension. It will, nevertheless, be a fact that a new dimension has been introduced and that that new dimension is what we now call the non-material. Be that as it may, the importance of establishing the existence of the non-material—of something which does not conform to the known laws of physics—is enormous. It establishes that basically the materialists are wrong and that the adherents of religion are right.

Let us examine this further in the context of survival of bodily death. A medium may give messages purporting to come from a deceased person, tending to establish the identity of that person, containing information known to the deceased, but unknown to the medium. As has been seen,[1] this may not conclusively prove survival, because there are always the possibilities of telepathy and precognition as logical alternatives. But, if they do not prove the identity of the alleged communicator, they certainly prove the abnormal sensitivity of the medium, for she has become possessed of information by some means other than the material. This in itself makes survival a much more probable hypothesis, for it indicates that there is something beyond the material, which in turn increases the probabilities that there is something in our make-up which is non-material and which, therefore, may well survive the dissolution of our material bodies. It is, in fact, strong corroboration of the Christian doctrine of the life everlasting, even though it be not conclusive proof of the truth of that doctrine.[2]

It may be argued that, for the committed Christian, the promises and power of the risen Christ should be sufficient guarantee without the help of adventitious aids. That is true, so far as it goes. But there are plenty of persons who are not committed Christians. For them this type of evidence may be exactly what is required to tip the balance and to turn them into committed Christians. Christianity can certainly survive without this sort of corroborative evidence; but the evidence can greatly strengthen Christianity's claims, confirm its adherents and confound its opponents.

Thus viewed, psychical research is the ally of religion in that it corroborates religion's basic claim that the non-material is a reality. This remains true, even for those who take the extreme view that psychic phenomena are diabolical, for the Devil himself, if he exists, is not material, but a spirit, and, whatever characteristics he may possess belong to the realm of the non-material.

It is a Christian tenet that there is a life after death. As has been seen, this is not conclusively proved by psychical research, though psychical research has made the truth of this belief more probable. Still less has psychical research established that life hereafter is life everlasting. On the evidence it is perfectly reasonable at times to believe that communications 'from the other side' in fact emanate from the source from which they purport to come, while still realising that the proof is not conclusive. But, while allowing that such a belief is reasonable, it must also be allowed that, even if, on a balance of probabilities, survival of bodily death be established, it does not follow that life hereafter is life everlasting. For all we know, from this type of evidence, such life may be as transitory as life on this earth. It may have its span and then be extinguished. Psychical research provides no evidence to the contrary. But psychical research does show that it is more probable that the Christian doctrine of the life everlasting is true. At the lowest estimate, psychical research shows that survival of bodily death is more probable than extinction, and some of the evidence shows that such survival is much more probable. This, for those who doubt, is a great leap forward. If survival of bodily death can be established, or even rendered probable, the great step forward has been taken. The next step, from mere survival to survival for all eternity, is a much smaller step. If survival at all occurs, it is not unreasonable to envisage it as going on for ever or as being but one further stage in a process which goes on for ever. This is all the more so having regard to our ignorance concerning the time-factor.[3] For all we know, time, as we understand it here, does not exist outside the material universe. It is, as it were, a framework for the material and can be shed together with the material. If however, it does exist outside the material universe, it may exist in a form very different from anything that we can envisage, and the words *eternal* and *everlasting* may have ceased to have meaning.

Be all this as it may, in establishing the existence of the non-material the contribution of psychical research to the cause of religion is enormous and it is not confined to the question of survival. Not the least of its contributions is in the extent to which it renders the Bible credible. It was materialism which for so many made the Biblical miracles so hard to believe. By demonstrating that the material is by no means all that is real, psychical research has rendered the miraculous far more credible. With the example of Dorothy Kerin[4] before us, we need no longer boggle at the Biblical miracles of healing. With the modern examples of ESP around us, we can the more readily accept our Lord's ESP[5] as literal fact and not as mythical hyperbole. In the light of modern cases of apparent possession,[6] we shall be more cautious in attributing the Biblical accounts of possession to the recorders' immaturity of understanding of matters medical. With the evidence which psychical research provides of nonmaterial forces, we can the more readily accept at their face-value the Biblical references to angels and to devils. With experience of apparitions in our own time, we can the more readily accept the literal truth of the accounts of our Lord's post-resurrection appearances. In short, in the light of psychical research, the scepticism engendered by Victorian materialism is cut down to size. The Bible is not proved to be true; but much of it is shown to be within the bounds of possibility, and the leap of faith is removed from the category of a foolhardy act by a blind man into that of a responsible decision by one who has weighed the *pros* and *cons*.

So much for the credit side. It is submitted that the assets there shown are considerable. What of the debit side?

For those who take the Bible seriously the most formidable condemnation of persons who have any truck with the psychic is based on certain passages in the Bible, and particularly in the Levitical writings. It is claimed that these and other passages utterly condemn psychic practices. In Deuteronomy,[7] for example, we read: 'When thou art come into the land which the Lord thy God giveth thee, thou shalt not learn to do after the abominations of those nations. There shall not be found among you anyone that maketh his son or daughter to pass through the fire, or that useth divination, or an observer of times, or an enchanter, or a witch, or a charmer, or a consulter with familiar spirits, or a wizard, or a necromancer. For all these things are an abomination unto the Lord: and because of these abominations the Lord thy God doth drive them out from before thee.'

In Exodus[8] it is written: 'Thou shalt not suffer a witch to live.'

In Leviticus[9] we find: 'Regard not them that have familiar spirits, neither seek after the wizards, to be defiled by them: I am the Lord your God.'

And again (Leviticus[10]): 'And the soul that turneth after such as have familiar spirits, and after wizards, to go a whoring after them, I will even set my face against that soul, and will cut him off from among his people.'

And again (Leviticus[11]): 'A man also or a woman that hath a familiar spirit, or that is a wizard, shall surely be put to death: they shall stone them with stones: their blood shall be upon them.'

Largely on these passages formidable arguments are presented against psychic practices. They are very well marshalled by Canon Stafford Wright in *Christianity and the Occult*[12] and they merit close scrutiny.

The first point to be observed is that one needs to go back to the Hebrew in order to understand what these passages mean, for the English translation is misleading. This book is no place for the examination in detail of the linguistic arguments;[13] it has been clearly done in *Nothing to Hide*.[14] Briefly, the argument amounts to this: that the prohibition in Exodus 18 and the condemnation in other passages are aimed at some practices which were fraudulent, at others which were sordid, and at any which were idolatrous. For example, the word which has been translated into English as *familiar spirit* is the Hebrew word, OB or OBH or OUV. This literally means *an empty wine-skin* or *wind-bag*, and became associated with the fraudulent practices of those who at a séance surreptitiously produced squeaks from it and indulged in ventriloquism for the deception of the sitter who had visited the 'medium' to obtain information from the dead. The type of necromancy at which the prohibition was aimed was not simple communication with the dead, but one which involved highly objectionable practices with corpses.

It is necessary also to take into account the background against which these items of the Law were promulgated. Though their origin purports to be about the time of the Exodus, in the form in which we have them they are several centuries later. They reflect the entry of the Jews into the Promised Land and their precarious foothold there, where they were under constant temptation to forget their vocation as the Chosen People and to flirt with, and even adopt, the religions and practices of the pagans around them. This was the idolatry against which both prophet and priest inveighed, and the psychic practices which came under their condemnation were inextricably entwined with these forms of idolatry. Against this background the weight to be attached to the prohibitions assumes a different proportion. Only the staunchest fundamentalist holds that the whole of the ancient Law is still to be observed. It is unlikely that today many would hold that the death-penalty should be imposed on a witch or a wizard in accordance with Exodus 22, 18 or Leviticus 20, 27, or on those who commit adultery in accordance with Leviticus 20, 10. It is equally unlikely that they would subscribe to the law that 'if an ox gore a man or a woman that they die, then the ox shall surely be stoned'.[15] We no longer feel it incumbent upon us to wear fringed garments[16] or to refrain from rounding the corners of our beards[17] or to abstain from eating pork.[18]

A degree of intelligent eclecticism is demanded in our acceptance of much in the Old Testament and the electic approach is consonant with the idea of progressive revelation. It is significant that the tone of the New Testament differs markedly from the ferocity of the Old Testament. The woman taken in adultery was merely told to sin no more.[19] Peter was told in a vision that all meats are clean.[20] 'An eye for an eye, and a tooth for a tooth'[21] gives place to foregiveness 'until seventy times seven'.[22] It is also relevant to our discussion to note that Simon the sorcerer was rebuked by Peter, not for sorcery, but for the offence of simony to which he has given his name, which is the attempt to buy spiritual gifts with money;[23] and it would seem that the damsel possessed with a spirit of divination who followed Paul about in Philippi grieved Paul, not by her gift, but by following him about and being a nuisance.[24]

In the Old Testament itself, there are plenty of indications that psychic gifts are not to be condemned. The prophets, who had these gifts in great measure, are held in great honour on account of them. Joseph not only interpreted dreams, but used a cup for the purpose of divination.[25] Daniel, a 'man greatly beloved' by the Lord,[26] received visions, interpreted dreams and (as we should say today) was credited with the possession of ESP of a high order. So was Elisha, and by means of it he was able to warn the King of Israel of the movements of the army of the King of Syria.[27]

It is clearly impossible to extract from the Bible a condemnation of everything psychic. Probably nobody who has considered the matter would attempt to do so, for it would involve the condemnation of an innate quality which, whether they enjoy it or not, some persons possess and which perhaps is latent in all persons. Any such condemnation would include our Lord himself within its ambit, for he exhibited ESP in a marked degree. The attack presumably is confined to certain psychic practices. But, even when the attack is thus limited, it is difficult to sustain. Witchcraft (at least of the black variety) is to be condemned, both because of the nature of its practices and because it is frankly satanic. But a God-fearing modern medium is not to be equated to the fraudulent medium condemned in Deuteronomy, chapter 18, nor with the sordid necromancer of those days. And, since some persons are endowed with psychic gifts, they cannot be criticised when these gifts manifest themselves spontaneously, and their owners can scarcely be condemned for using, or even developing, them.

But that is not to suggest that the Bible is to be ignored. One thing emerges clearly from an over-all reading of it, namely, that our God-given talents, whatever they be, should be used to the glory of the God who has given them. To pervert them to other purposes may well be to fall within the Levitical condemnations. A good discretion is required, and wariness is to be commended. There are times when St John's warning is apposite:[28] 'Beloved, believe not every spirit, but try the spirits whether they are of God: because many false prophets are gone out into the world. Hereby know ye the spirit of God: Every spirit that confesseth that Jesus Christ is come in the flesh is of God: and every spirit that confesseth not that Jesus Christ is come in the flesh is not of God: and this is that spirit of antichrist, whereof ye have heard that it should come: and even now already is it in the world.'

On a more practical plane, those who eschew all psychic practices often claim that it renders its practitioners unstable and opens the door through which undesirable forces may take possession of them. The claim is probably exaggerated; but it is not without some substance. Most certainly those who are not by nature of a stable equilibrium should avoid, so far as they can, all contact with the psychic. This is not always easy, for a person may well be both schizophrenic and also endowed with psychic gifts which force themselves to the surface. But certainly the unstable should try to keep themselves free from psychic influences. The danger of possession is real, though slight. It can occur, or, at least, it looks as though it does sometimes occur. But when one has regard to the large number of practising spiritualists who do their best to encourage psychic manifestations and who exhibit no sign of being possessed (other than when actually in trance or semi-trance), the danger is seen to be of no great proportion. When, however, it does occur, it can be devastating. It is, therefore, sound practical policy to warn persons, especially the young, not to play about light-heartedly with the ouija-board or with anything else pertaining to the psychic. For the serious psychical researcher it is a calculated risk. As in other fields of exploration, it is a risk which is justified, and, as in many a field of research, without risk no advance can be made. Apart from the intrinsic value of the study of the psychic for its own sake, it has its immediate practical value. There are those who are worried by psychic manifestations, whether they be of apparitions or poltergeists or anything else, and who require to be reassured and helped. Reassurance and help can be given only by those who have made some study of the psychic, inadequate though at present their knowledge be.

Exorcism can prove beneficial to the patient; but, like any other operation, it should not be attempted by those who have not acquainted themselves, so far as possible, with the evil which they are seeking to remove, and this can be achieved only by a study of the subject.

Another obvious danger, but one which is seldom mentioned, is the danger of being frightened. Psychic manifestations can be alarming, and fright can be very traumatic.

But the greatest danger of all, to my mind, is one which is never mentioned. It is a subtle one and it is a spiritual danger rather than a psychical or physical one. It is the danger of triviality. It is the danger into which those persons fall who are constantly seeking communication with the departed. Apart from the very doubtful nature of many of these alleged communications, and apart from the utter lack of value which so often they exhibit, the danger lies in the recipient's resting content with these trivialities and ceasing to seek a deeper and real communion with God. That is the basic danger. But it is one which overflows into other channels. It can lead to an abandonment of the search for truth by other more orthodox and more strenuous and more profitable means, calling for a measure of self-discipline. In can lead to a dangerous reliance on supposed and unsure guidance from beyond the grave in matters affecting this life, with a consequent surrender of initiative in those mundane matters which are committed to our own care and judgement. It provides in fact a meretricious easy option, lulling its victims into a false feeling of security. The consequent malaise can manifest itself in a number of different ways; but basically it stems from an often unavowed, but nevertheless real, displacing of God from his proper position of centrality in our lives; and *that* is the true idolatry, rightly condemned in the Levitical scriptures. And, for all we know, actively promoted by Satan as a subtle and powerful weapon wherewith to deflect souls from God.

Let us now take a look at our balance-sheet. So far as the cause of religion is concerned, we can now see that the psychic provides entries on both the credit and the debit side. It is in some respects an ally of religion. In other respects it can be inimical to religion. Our assessment of where the balance lies is of necessity a value-judgement. It must be clear by now that my own assessment is that the psychic, properly regarded and properly approached, is a powerful ally to religion though no substitute for it. Whether this assessment be right or wrong, the psychic is, for good or ill, a factor which both physics and religion must take into account. It must, therefore, be studied. To say that it must be properly approached is not to differentiate it from anything else which is potentially powerful. Fire and water can be very dangerous as well as very beneficial, and experiments with them should be conducted with circumspection. The same is true of investigations into the psychic. It is not for dabblers, and the serious researcher should be circumspect. As a counsel of perfection, he should be God-fearing; but, whether or not he acknowledges the Creator, he should approach his task with that reverence for the wonders of Creation and for the truth which informs every true scientist whether he be theist, atheist or agnostic.

'Magna est veritas et praevalebit.'

NOTES

Chapter 2

1. Clairvoyance is the faculty of seeing something mentally, and clairaudience is the faculty of hearing something mentally, in both cases without the aid of the physical senses.

2. John 1. 45–51. It is fashionable in some quarters to question the factuality of the incidents recorded in the Fourth Gospel. While it is clear that the author was concerned to marshal his facts in a manner which would best underline those aspects of Jesus which he was anxious to present to his readers, there is little to suggest that the events related were pure fiction without any factual foundation.

Chapter 3

1. For examples of dreams which frustrate their own fulfilment by warning the dreamer of danger see *Over the High Wall*, by J. B. Priestley, pp. 101 *et seq.*

Chapter 5

1. Extensively examined by G. N. M. Tyrrell in his *Myers Memorial Lecture* for the SPR (Gerald Duckworth & Co., 1943, revised 1953).

2. *An Adventure* (1st edn, 1911, Macmillan & Co. Ltd., London). A large volume of criticism and discussion of this case has followed, much of it in the *Journals* of the SPR, and further additions of *An Adventure* have appeared.

3. See especially *Can We Explain the Poltergeist?* by A. R. G. Owen (Helin Press, New York, 1964).

Chapter 6

1. Ecclesiastes 12. 6, 7. The more prosaic exegesis of this passage is that it is a reference to the silver chain from which was pendant the golden lamp, possibly connected with Zechariah, 4. 2, 3.

2. A list of his books is given on p. 88 of *Life, Death and Psychical Research* (Rider & Co., London) and an article by him, beginning at p. 66 of that book, contains an abbreviated account of a number of cases.

3. *Op. cit.*

4. See pp. 43 and 44.

5. Job 19. 26.

6. 1 Cor. 15. 35 *et seq.*

Chapter 7

1. See Chapter 8, pp. 76 and 77.

2. *Human Personality and the Survival of Bodily Death* (Longman, London, reprinted 1939), vol. 1, p. 553. For many further instances see *Abnormal Hypnotic Phenomena* (4 vols.), by Eric J. Dingwall, D.Sc. (J. & A. Churchill Ltd., London, 1967 and 1968).

Chapter 8

1. See pp. 31–33.

2. An interesting account of this in the early part of the nineteenth century is to be found in *The Manners and Customs of the Modern Egyptians*, by E. W. Lowe (Everyman ed., no. 274 *et seq.*; published by Dent). It would seem possible that telepathy was involved in these instances.

3. See *Thirty Years of Psychical Research* by Richet (translated by Stanley de Brath, W. Collins & Co. Ltd, 1923, Glasgow, Melbourne and Auckland), p. 130.

4. That is, in 1974.

5. See *inter alia*, in *New Horizons* (Canada) for July 1974 two articles by Dr A. R. G. Owen, pp. 164 *et seq.* and pp. 172 *et seq.* See also SPR *Journal*, vol. 47, No. 762. See also the *New Scientist* for 17 October 1974, p. 170 and the other reports there cited. See also *Nature* for 18 October 1974 (vol. 251, No. 5476), pp. 559 and 602.

6. Otherwise known as psychokinesis (PK).

Chapter 9

1. Genesis 1. 26.
2. Genesis 1. 26, 28.
3. Ephesians 4. 25.
4. *Dorothy Kerin*, by Dorothy Musgrave Arnold (Hodder and Stoughton).
5. E.g. my own Guild church of St Mary Abchurch, in the City of London, has regular services once a month. The Guild of St Raphael exists to further the ministry of healing. Some dioceses have appointed a Director of Healing.
6. Mark 16. 15–18. This passage is recognised as a later addition to the Gospel, but it accords with much else in the Bible and reflects the understanding of the early Church.
7. John 14. 12.
8. Mark 16. 18.
9. James 5. 14.
10. Genesis 1. 31.
11. 1 Cor. 12. 9.
12. Luke 9. 50.
13. Matthew 12. 24–28.
14. Book of Common Prayer.
15. *Pace* Dr Louis Rose, a sympathetic agnostic concerning healing, whose book, *Faith Healing* (Penguin Books) provides a useful antidote to too ready an acceptance of some of the claims made on behalf of less orthodox methods of healing.
16. John 11.
17. Luke 7. 12–17.
18. Matthew 13. 58. For lack of confidence or faith on the part of the healer, as distinct from on the part of the patient (in exorcism), see Matthew 17. 20. Cf. also Mark 9, 23 and 24.
19. Had the scope of this book permitted, a full exegesis of the Biblical references in this chapter would have been desirable. See Preface.

Chapter 10

1. Matthew 8. 28–34. Mark 5. 1–29. Luke 8. 26–39.
2. Matthew 17. 14–21; Mark 9. 17–29; Luke 9. 37–43.
3. Matthew 9. 32; Luke 11. 14.
4. Acts 16. 16–18.

5. See Chapter 5 for Hauntings.
6. i.e. since about 1960.
7. Ephesians 6. 12.
8. See Chapter 4.
9. See *The Dissociation of Personality*, by Morton Prinel, M.D.C. (Longmans, Green & Co., New York, 1906.)
10. Cf. Matthew 17. 21: 'This kind goeth not out but by prayer and fasting' (to quote but one example).
11. England, 1974.
12. See the *Washington Post* for 20 August, 1949; also the *Times Herald* (Washington) of the same date; also the *Evening Star* (Washington) for 19 August, 1949.
13. Matthew 12. 43–45.
14. *Exorcism*, ed. by Dom Robert Petipierre (SPCK).
15. But see p. 100.

Chapter 11

1. Chapter 4.
2. Such survival is not necessarily proof of *everlasting* life. See what follows.
3. See Chapter 3.
4. See p. 82 *et seq.*
5. See p. 8.
6. See Chapter 10.
7. 18. 9–17.
8. 22. 18.
9. 19. 31.
10. 20. 6.
11. 20. 27.
12. Scripture Union (1971).
13. Nor am I fitted to conduct such an examination.
14. By the Revd Leonard Argyle, B.D. (Churches' Fellowship for Psychical and Spiritual Studies, 1970).
15. Exodus 21. 28.
16. Deuteronomy 22. 12; Numbers 15. 38; Deuteronomy 22. 12.
17. Leviticus 19. 27. and 21. 5.
18. Leviticus 11. 7. For some reason, which he does not explain, Canon Stafford Wright is irritated by this argument (op. cit., p. 119).

19. John 8. 3–11.
20. Acts 10. 9 *et seq.*; 11. 1–10.
21. Matthew 5. 38; Exodus 21. 14; Leviticus 24. 20. Deuteronomy 19. 21.
22. Matthew 18. 22.
23. Acts 8. 9–24.
24. Acts 16. 16–18.
25. Genesis 44. 1–5.
26. Daniel 10. 11.
27. 11 Kings 6. 8–12.
28. 1 John 4. 1–3.

SUGGESTIONS FOR FURTHER READING

THERE is now a vast literature on or connected with psychical research, and the reader who comes fresh to the subject may well feel at a loss to know where to turn, if, after this introductory book, he wishes to pursue the subject further, for the references given in the body of the text do not of themselves indicate a systematic course of reading.

There is a temptation to begin with one of the great classics, such as *Human Personality and its Survival of Bodily Death*, by F. W. H. Myers (1903, Longmans, and, in an abridged version, by Longmans, Green & Co., 1919), or *Phantasms of the Living*, by Gurney, Myers and Podmore (London, 1886, published in a shorter edition, New York, 1961), or *Our Sixth Sense*, by Charles Richet (translated, 1927, Rider), and they are well worth reading. But some progress has been made since they were written, and the reader will more quickly obtain a better picture by starting with some more recent books.

The Sixth Sense and *The Infinite Hive* both by Rosalind Heywood (Pan Books), provide an excellent introduction as does also *Life, Death and Psychical Research*, a symposium by a number of authors, published by Rider & Co., on behalf of the Churches' Fellowship for Psychical and Spiritual Studies.

Thereafter, for an indication of how experiments may be conducted, the reader could turn to *From Anecdote to Experiment*, by Robert Thouless, D.Sc. (Routledge & Kegan Paul, London).

After that (and before reading the older classics), he should learn something of the recent history of the subject, which will be found in *The Founders of Psychical Research*, by Alan Gauld (Routledge, London).

For precognition and the time factor, *An Experiment with Time* (Faber, 1927) and (with more mathematics) *The Serial Universe* (Faber), both by J. W. Dunne, should be read. There is also an interesting article by Dr J. E. Orme in the SPR *Journal* (vol. 4, No. 760, June, 1974), and another by H. A. C. Dobbs, entitled *Time and Extrasensory Perception*, in the *Proceedings of the SPR* (vol. 54, Part 197, 1965).

For apparitions, there is W. H. Salter's *Ghosts and Apparitions* (1938, G. Bell & Sons, Ltd) and G. N. M. Tyrrell's *Apparitions* (1942, published by Gerald Duckworth & Co. Ltd for the SPR); while for poltergeist-manifestations Dr A. R. G. Owen has written *Can We Explain the Poltergeist?* (Helix Press, New York, 1964).

Dr Robert Crookall has written extensively on out-of-the-body experiences, and among his books are *The Study and Practice of Astral Projection* (1960) and *More Astral Projections* (1964), both published by the Aquarian Press. Muldoon and Carrington have written *The Phenomena of Astral Projection* (1969) and *The Projection of the Astral Body* (both published by Rider & Co.), while Celia Green has contributed *Lucid Dreams* and *Out-of-the-Body Experiences* (both published in 1968 by the Institute of Psychophysical Research). In addition, Sir Cyril Burt's Myers Memorial Lecture on

Psychology and Psychical Research (1968, SPR) should be read.

There are many books, both psychical and medical, on hypnosis. A good beginning may be made with Eric Cudden's *Hypnosis: Its Meaning and Practice* (Bell, 1957).

For a more philosophical approach to psychical research there is Arthur Koestler's *The Roots of Coincidence* (Hutchinson, 1972), and the late Professor C. D. Broad's Myers Memorial Lecture (SPR, 1958) on *Personal Identity and Survival*, and his *Lectures on Psychical Research* (Routledge & Kegan Paul, 1962).

The Palm Sunday Case, by Jean Balfour (1960, *Proceedings of the SPR*, vol. 52, p. 79), provides a fascinating account of alleged messages from beyond the grave over a long period of time, in their design seeming to indicate a planned experiment from that side in order to impress those on this side, and, incidentally, of interest to historians for the light it sheds on the life and character of Arthur, Lord Balfour, to whom the communications were primarily addressed.

During his many years of research in America J. B. Rhine has produced a number of books and papers, among them *Extrasensory Perception* (Boston, 1934) and *The Reach of the Mind* (Faber, 1948), while Louisa E. Rhine has contributed *Hidden Channels of the Mind* (William Sloane Associates, New York).

For a theological assessment adverse to many psychic practices see *Christianity and the Occult*, by Canon J. Stafford Wright (Scripture Union, 1971); and for a theological refutation of these views see *Nothing to Hide*, by the Revd Leonard Argyle (Churches' Fellowship for Psychical and Spiritual Studies, 1970). See also the views of the late Dean W. R. Matthews expressed in his Myers

Memorial Lecture (*Proceedings of the SPR*, vol. 46. Part
161), *Psychical Research and Theology*.

There are many books on the spiritual and psychical
aspects of healing. A useful one with which to begin,
because it gives so many Biblical references, is *The Healing Ministry*, by Bertram E. Woods, a Methodist minister
(Rider & Co., 1961), followed by *The Heart of Healing*,
by George Bennett, an Anglican priest (Arthur James
Ltd., 1971). A very thorough examination of Anglican
practices with regard to healing is given by a Roman
Catholic in *The Ministry of Healing in the Church of
England*, by Charles W. Gusmer (Mayhew-McCrimmon
Group, 1975). A sympathetic agnostic consideration is
given from the medical angle by Louis Rose in *Faith
Healing* (Penguin Books, 1971). The biography of
Dorothy Kerin, by Dorothy Musgrove Arnold (Hodder
& Stoughton, 1965), should also be read.

Closely related to healing is exorcism. The following
is a list of recent books on the subject:

*Exorcism: The Findings of a Commission Convened
by the [then] Bishop of Exeter*, edited by Dom Robert
Petitpierre, OSB (SPCK, 1972).

But Deliver Us from Evil, by John Richards (Darton,
Longman & Todd, 1974).

The Exorcist and the Possessed, by Christopher Neil-
Smith (James Pike, Ltd).

Experiences of a Present Day Exorcist, by Donald
Oman (Kimber, 1970).

The Society for Psychical Research has a well-stocked
library at 1 Adam and Eve Mews, London, W.8, and
its *Journal* and its *Proceedings* provide a rich source of
information and comment on almost every aspect of the
psychic.

INDEX